Remodel Your Kitchen!

WITHOUT GOING
BONKERS OR BROKE

Remodel Your Kitchen!

WITHOUT GOING BONKERS OR BROKE

A Step-by-Step Guide to a Stress-Free
Renovation and the Kitchen of Your Dreams

Jim Molinelli

the "Remodeling Professor"

ISBN-10: 0578813459
ISBN 13: 978-0-578-81345-5

For your non-kitchen projects, read:

Remodel!

Without Going Bonkers or Broke

"Very, very informative. Well written and easy to understand. I enjoyed reading this book from the first page." Sandra Altizio – New Jersey

"This is the most comprehensive book on the subject that I have ever seen!" Janine Wooten – Realtor & Real Estate Investor – Florida

"I would label Jim Molinelli's book 'a Bible' for anyone considering a remodeling project. Use it as a handy reference." Lilly Brock – Retired Interior Designer & Remodeler – Washington

"A first-rate guide to remodeling your home written as if the author was sitting across from you at your dining room table answering all of your questions." Ted Sugges – New Jersey

"Jim Molinelli is the American Mike Holmes." Lisa Schatz – California

"This was easily the most practical 'how-to' book I've ever read." Adam Drummond – Wagga Wagga, Australia

"Remodel changed everything for me. I now have real confidence where I had serious doubts before." Laura Lynn – Tennessee

"My confidence is sky-high now. I'm so excited about planning my project that I could burst!" Terrica Simmons – Mississippi

"People terrified of being ripped off by remodelers are going to LOVE this. I know. I was one." Dr. Marlena Corcoran – CEO – NYC

————◆————

The Readers' Favorite
2017 GOLD MEDAL WINNER

Sometimes...
you still have questions or concerns,
even after reading a book like this.

Now you can...

Ask the
Remodeling Professor!

Jim offers **1-on-1 video coaching calls** and
gives **clear answers and action steps**
for your specific situation!

———◆———

Jim is an impartial remodeling expert,
a life-long industry insider, and
his only interest is your success!

———◆———

SCHEDULE A CALL NOW:
www.RemodelingProfessor.com/call

Contents

Dedication

I dedicate this book to my son Timothy who sees and experiences this world through the filters of Autism and cognitive impairment.

His slow but constant advances in language, communications, and human interaction are hard fought and well deserved.

He inspires me to always strive to become more than I am.

Acknowledgments

I must thank Jeff Hilderman, Liz Nolley Tillman, Jason Stuck, Michele Laine, and Eevi Jones for their deep friendships and assistance with this book and all my entrepreneurial endeavors. I would not be where I am today without them.

Once again, thanks to Chandler Bolt and his fine company, Self-Publishing School for an excellent writing and publishing environment. Their superb author community is without equal.

To my many clients and students, I owe immense thanks. I learned what I know about design and remodeling from your projects. Without you I'd never have come to this place and time. Thank you.

Finally, I could not have written this book or built this business without the endless support and encouragement of my wonderful wife, Shawn, and my two great kids Tim and Ann. I'm a very lucky man.

Author's Note

I decided to write my first book *Remodel!* **Without Going Bonkers or Broke** in the summer of 2016 after having taught my how-to remodel classes to homeowners for more than a dozen years at the local college. I joined an online publishing school (Self-PublishingSchool.com) and the book was published on Amazon in February of 2017.

I met and have become fast friends with quite a few of my fellow authors from that time. Many of them are now full-time authors and entrepreneurs. Of course, they asked me continuously "What will your next book be?" I had no plans to write any more books, and I told them so. I was focused on building my business and developing my online remodeling classes for homeowners.

Now it seems that I'm the poster child for the phrase "Never say never". My first book was so well received that with a bit of urging from my business mastermind group, I decided to write the book you're holding now.

It's been an absolutely wonderful experience. As I worked on this book in earnest, that same excitement and enthusiasm I had with the first book returned. I realized that everyone wants a kitchen they love and are proud to show off. Now that can be a reality for anyone that takes the time to follow this simple method.

I'm once again indebted to so many who encouraged and supported this effort.

This book turned out so well that I now plan a brand-new edition of the original book to bring it up to the standard of this volume.

My goal throughout my architecture and remodeling careers was, and remains today as the Remodeling Professor, to help people improve their homes and improve their lives. When you walk into your new kitchen each morning, I want you to smile and say to yourself, "Damn, I'm so glad I did this project!"

Then I'll know I made a difference.

Jim Molinelli
November 2020

Introduction

Introduction

Remodeling projects can easily spiral out of control, lowering project quality, increasing costs dramatically, and even ending in lawsuits.

So, when homeowners planning to remodel are scared or intimidated by this seemingly overwhelming process, it's no surprise. To anyone outside the industry, the process does seem overwhelming.

Despite the huge number of decisions and details involved in a kitchen remodel, it needn't overwhelm or intimidate you. In fact, some simple, focused preparation will improve both your confidence and your final results.

I believe that every homeowner can get results they cherish and love to show off. All you need is some unbiased guidance and a little pre-project planning.

Can you imagine a kitchen that will make your days easier and your life better?

Just follow the step-by-step process I share in this book, and your new dream kitchen will be a raving success.

About a year ago I met with a former student and client. While we were talking, she floored me with this statement: **"Jim, every day when I walk in there, I fall in love with my kitchen all over again"**. I bet that you'd like to have results that leave you feeling that way.

Remodel Your Kitchen! is your kitchen renovation roadmap. It will help you navigate the remodeling minefield, avoiding the costly mistakes that derail so many projects. You will successfully plan and coordinate your kitchen renovation—from initial inspiration through signing a contract.

The very best part is that you will also save money. Lots of money. My insider tips and techniques can literally save you thousands.

You will fail only if you DO NOT follow the proven path that I have prepared for you. The results of your kitchen renovation are now in your hands, literally.

Remodeling is an exciting adventure. And with this straightforward process, high-quality results are assured.

I chose this career so I could help people fall in love with their homes again.

Are you ready to begin? Your kitchen remodeling journey starts now!

Chapter 1

How to Use This Book

Okay. Maybe this chapter title is a little odd. After all, everyone knows how to use a book. You read to the end of the page, then go to the next page and do it again, right?

But, because of the cost of kitchen remodeling and the need to get it right the first time, it's important that you know what to expect from this book.

The book is divided into five sections. The first three sections cover the 3 pillars of any successful remodel: **CLARIFY**, **CONSULT** and **CHOOSE**. These sections lay the foundation for a successful project by boosting your remodeling IQ. CLARIFY gets you prepared to seize and maintain control of your project. CONSULT examines the different types of designers and remodelers available, so you consider the ones best suited for your kitchen project. CHOOSE helps you identify, interview, rank, negotiate, and sign with your ideal remodeler.

The fourth section is about **SAVING MONEY**. There are techniques you can apply right from the outset (even while you are preplanning) that can literally save you thousands. I also mention methods to avoid wasting and losing money.

The fifth section **THROUGH MY EYES** is a deep-dive into the key decisions involved in all kitchen projects. You'll learn much of the logic and many insider tips needed to make key kitchen-related decisions in advance. You'll resolve which functions and features your kitchen solution must deliver to be successful.

The process in this book literally takes you from concept to contract.

What's not included is anything about the construction phase. Why? Because, the end results are already pre-determined by the quality of your preparation and your decisions prior to signing the contract.

Nothing done during construction can save a poorly planned project.

And nothing done during construction can ruin a well-planned project.

For this reason, I focus on the 5 portions of the process that you control personally (Clarify, Consult, Choose, Saving Money, Through My Eyes). When you get those right, a solid, high-quality result is automatic.

I'd like to clarify two things before we begin your remodeling journey: This is not a DIY book and it is not a picture book.

The book is only and specifically for those who plan to hire professionals to produce their project, and that particular process.

I understand that a lack of photos frustrates some readers. But I've made my best effort to explain the kitchen remodeling process simply and carefully. I tried to remain conversational and entertaining while covering the ins and outs of planning and coordinating a professional kitchen remodel. I have included a handful of illustrations, charts, and graphics that were required to get some key points across.

Section 1:
CLARIFY

The most common mistake made by homeowners when they remodel is that they enter the process unprepared or underprepared. That's typically because they are unfamiliar with the remodeling process, or they find it scary and intimidating.

This first Section of the book (Clarify) provides you a simple, step-by-step process to eliminate any fear or intimidation you may feel. You will learn exactly how to create a Project Packet—an item I created for my personal clients that lets anyone successfully launch a remodeling project. Your Project Packet combines specific project-related information that fuels your remodeling journey, properly preparing you and your hired team for a successful experience.

The Project Packet helps you clarify exactly what your new kitchen should (and should not) include and accomplish. Clarifying your project vision in this manner gives critical insight to your professionals, so their clever solutions provide joy and delight in addition to addressing your crucial needs.

You probably don't yet know all that you want or need in your new kitchen. Don't worry! A little inspired guidance along with some deliberate thought, and your kitchen project will take shape surprisingly fast.

Chapter 2

Remodeling Mindset

Mayhem. There, I said it. The nine hundred-pound gorilla has been called out. What kind of book on remodeling would this be if it didn't mention horror-story results? A remodeling book that fails to acknowledge that *most professional remodeling projects fail to meet the needs, goals, or aspirations of the homeowner* would be a fairy tale.

But I didn't write, and you didn't buy, a fairy tale. I intend to help you plan and coordinate an awesome kitchen renovation.

Remodel Your Kitchen! Doesn't pull any punches or beat around the bush. To be very clear, you, the homeowner, hold the fate of your remodeling project in your hands. How your kitchen turns out is totally up to you.

If that shocks or scares you a little bit… good! It should. Because you never want to spend tens of thousands of hard-earned dollars on a project which fails to satisfy **your** expectations. That's my definition of a failed project.

The primary goal of any remodeling project is to meet the needs of the homeowner. Period. Once that is accomplished a clever arrangement or an upscale look are wonderful bonuses—but those should never be the primary motivation.

In my long career as an architect and design-build remodeler, I've observed thousands of remodeling projects. I always paid particular attention when I saw or learned of projects that had "failed." I discovered that the owner typically made the mistakes that caused the project to fail!

What did they do?

There are three errors that homeowners make regularly that can hurt, alter, sabotage, or ruin their projects. Each one of these mistakes is crucial and can derail any project. I'll carefully explain each one and how to easily avoid them later. But for now, let's simply say that the majority of failed remodeling projects are the result of an incorrect "mindset" by the owner as they set out on their remodeling journey.

You may wonder how the mindset of a homeowner can sabotage the result of a remodeling project. Read the three statements that follow. These exceptionally common thoughts each describe a different type of owner whose projects fail:

- I haven't got a clue what to do…
- I know what I'm doing—I'll figure things out and it will be okay.
- I watch HGTV all the time—how hard can this be?

The first statement (I haven't got a clue) is easily the most common homeowner thought, and it seems pretty harmless on the surface. I suppose these homeowners recognize their lack of remodeling knowledge and they decide to call in a professional to help them, *hoping* that they get sound advice from the ideal person or company. But by calling on random contractors while the homeowners are still unprepared, they've already given away control of their project to their "professional." The best-case result at that point is an "okay" solution based on that remodeler's experience with other customers. Essentially their design solution will be based on other people's needs and goals. And that's true only if the remodeler selected is a high-quality professional. This situation is more likely to result in a nightmare experience if their random call attracts the wrong candidate. This outcome resides wholly on the quality and skills of the professional chosen, simply because the owner relinquishes control of their project.

With the second statement (I know what I'm doing), owners often fail to seek or accept prudent advice from the professionals they meet with. You would be shocked to learn how many homeowners simply want "what they want" and refuse to listen to their paid professionals. In this case, results are often disastrous and expensive. These homeowners almost never see that they personally doomed their project to fail, and they blame the bad results on their remodeler.

With the third statement (I watch HGTV), you need to know that TV remodeling is just entertainment. Calling it "reality" TV is a huge mistake! In real-life remodeling, everything takes longer, costs more, and is much more difficult than what is portrayed on television. The HGTV-affected homeowner is virtually assured of a poor or disappointing experience, with seemingly huge increases in production time and price compared to TV projects. Even the occasional excellent project can be tarnished simply because they held false hopes and expectations related to timing or cost.

Projects of owners with the wrong remodeling mindset seldom live up to expectations. With kitchen renovations costing so much money, any result that is not delightfully satisfying is a failure in my opinion. So what can be done?

For now, just understand that when you remodel with the right mindset, you can eliminate mayhem, and your sound decisions steer the project in a successful direction. You can build a team of trustworthy professionals that want to help you accomplish your unique kitchen dreams and meet your budget without major cost overruns.

My confession to you is that most of my clients came from mindset group one above (I have no idea what to do). They were very lucky to hire someone capable of leading them step-by-step through the remodeling process. Truth be told, a large number of spectacular architects and remodelers are out there just waiting for a call from someone like you, hoping to work together on a top-quality project of which everyone is proud.

Yet, only the best-trained and most experienced professionals take the time to determine the owner's true core needs so the solutions they propose actually address those needs. This is super important because without knowing the owner's goals for a project, the very best any professional can do is design a generic modification based on their experiences with other families. And those solutions are not likely to meet the current homeowner's core needs.

This is why **you** need an accurate grasp of the fundamentals of your project before you lift a finger to ask for help. When you help your designer and contractor clearly understand your needs and you can show them "your vision," then half the battle is already won. But I'm getting a little bit ahead of myself.

So what is the proper remodeling mindset—the one that will lead to a partnership with a top designer or remodeler and generate results you love?

It is the boss mindset. That's right. Imagine yourself as the big boss of a large company. You have a huge corner office with a spectacular view. You have an assistant outside tending to your calls and appointments while you sit at your massive desk. You are surrounded by full bookcases, loads of awards, and the obligatory bragging wall full of "grip and grin" photos. Your job is to plan the future of the company, and you're the captain of the ship.

Today you're busy pondering a crucial new hire. You've decided it's time to bring in a specialist to help you with a brand-new project that has huge potential. You're mulling over this new position. The new specialist will have a set of important responsibilities that come with the job, so you're reviewing your expectations about their future performance. You're also debating how much you're willing to pay to the ideal candidate. Additionally, you make some notes about the amount and type of experience they must have before you will even consider interviewing them. You also list some of the unique skills and qualifications the job requires. Finally, if they meet your initial requirements, during the interview you will need to verify their character and determine if they have a team-based attitude.

Can you see yourself in that chair, behind that huge desk as that boss? Well, that is the mindset you should assume when you're preparing to remodel a kitchen.

Be the Boss!

You are *the Boss* of your project—with a capital B. You are about to make the most important hire of your career as a homeowner, and your job posting must be as accurate and complete as possible. You will interview only the most successful, pre-qualified applicants for your job. So, your job posting should be used as a filter—to eliminate all but the very best candidates.

Sound farfetched? It's not. What's more, you maintain this "Boss" mindset throughout the remodeling process.

Obviously, your designer and contractor will know far more than you do about remodeling kitchens since that's their specific field of expertise. Think about it. In most businesses, the specialist employees know far more about the details of their specific jobs than the boss does. But an outstanding boss hires the most qualified team players they can find, sets the direction they should go, keeps everyone focused on a successful outcome, and trusts the employees to perform at their best.

There is no doubt that your kitchen project will be guided by your employees' expert advice and input. But they remain the employee, and you remain the Boss—you retain the final say at all times. You monitor all project performance and progress according to the job description and the employment contract.

Even if you have never been a boss before, please don't worry. This book helps you understand the best possible mindset for a successful kitchen renovation.

Just remember, remodeling should be an exciting and life-improving experience! And as *the Boss*, you seize and maintain control of your project from beginning to end.

So have your assistant hold your calls, and let's start planning your kitchen remodeling project and building your Project Packet!

Critical Remodeling Mistake #1

Don't begin the remodeling process without being fully prepared.

Jumping into the remodeling process by calling in professionals without first doing your own project preparations is the first of three critical mistakes often made by homeowners.

Without realizing it, they hand over control of the remodeling project to someone else before having even a simple plan or preparations in place. The risk of a project becoming a horror story is now remarkably high based on the unknown character, quality and skill of the company partnered with.

Considering the dollar amounts involved in most remodeling projects, and how hard we work to earn our money, this is a simply unacceptable error.

Chapter 3

Create A Project Packet

The chapters in this section help you to fully prepare *before* you contact the professionals that help your dream kitchen come to life. This is necessary regardless of who designs or constructs your project. Even highly-skilled architects and kitchen remodeling specialists thrive with clients who can clearly explain the goals for their kitchen. Otherwise, the best they can provide is a generic solution based on their experiences, that may or may not meet your needs.

This section will help you CLARIFY your goals and project details, collecting them into a Project Packet. The Project Packet will help everyone on your remodeling team clearly understand your vision, and stay on the same page.

Your **Project Packet** describes the goals and known details of your ideal new kitchen. The Project Packet sets the overall scope of the project, describes your unique needs, and sets your budget, among other things. Presenting this information to your professional partners allows them to better help you succeed.

When creating your Project Packet, you will need to make a project file so you can organize (and not lose track of) all your important kitchen information. You'll collect loads of ideas, notes, photos, and helpful website URLs and all sorts of fun information as you plan your kitchen. So, take a moment to figure out how you will store and organize your remodeling materials and information.

You will have lots of kitchen-related materials and options (appliances, flooring choices, cabinet door style preference and finish, etc.). You will have an assortment of different types of information including pictures and brochures, websites, notes and lists, computer files, and lots of digital photos.

Choose one location where you store everything, and a method to keep it organized—so you can find the items when you need them! It doesn't matter if you store them in a physical file folder system, or as digital information on your computer. But heed this warning: Don't store this information in multiple forms or in multiple locations. Assemble everything in one location and keep it organized.

A first-rate Project Packet is the biggest predictor of your project's success.

If you prepare an excellent Project Packet—one that clearly communicates your remodeling goals and expectations—then your probability of remodeling success increases dramatically. Your kitchen designers and remodeling professionals will have a detailed understanding of your vision, allowing them to design a creative solution that meets or maybe even exceeds your expectations.

Here are two insider tips that will help make your Project Packet preparations a little more effective.

Action Item #1:

Get your laptop ready (or your tablet, or a pad and pencil) so you can make notes as we start going through the Project Packet elements: the Elevator Pitch, the Need List, the Wish List, the Budget, and the Project Scope. Make whatever project-related notes you wish as you read through the information the first time. Keep these all together in the same place, since they will become part of your Project Packet.

As you reach the individual Action Items for each Project Packet element, reread that section and perform the prescribed task. Afterward, read through your own first draft of the Packet sections and keep working the material into the best shape possible. Add new information and make edits as you learn more. The Project Packet is a work in progress, so stick with it.

Give your Project Packet your full focus and effort. The quality of the information you put together here significantly improves the quality of the custom design solution your professionals can deliver.

Make Your Photos Count!

Take photos of all the parts and pieces you might want to capture and replicate in your kitchen project. Wherever you find them, snap a digital photo of each part, each material, and each look.

Then, to *make them count*, type or write a very clear note on each image so you and your design professional know precisely what to replicate from each image.

If it was a type of window you want to use, great. If it's a particular style of window seat, awesome. If it's an idea for an island layout you love, that's ideal. And if it's the style of cabinet door you want to use, perfect!

Just be sure you note the exact thing you want the designer to notice, understand, and incorporate, so all the other details in the photo can be disregarded!

Action Item #2:

Visit the website Houzz (www.Houzz.com) and make a free account. Then you can create different "Idea Books" where you can save (and annotate) images searched from their millions of project photos. Being able to type notes about each image is a huge benefit that allows you to recall exactly why you were inspired by each image.

It's fun to search HOUZZ and collect photos that illustrate the little bits and pieces of a kitchen solution you'd like to see in your home. Later, when the time comes, you can even share your idea books with your architect or design professional.

You can make multiples as well, in case you want one just for islands, or mudrooms, etc.

Be Observant!

Everywhere you go, start paying attention to the details!

When you visit the homes of others, look at their kitchens and see what inspires you (good or bad).

When you're out shopping, look at tile and the designs that can be done with it.

When you visit home centers, go up and down aisles that you never visit, and see all the items they sell that you might want to consider in your new kitchen.

Inspiration is everywhere! Be observant and be sure to take great digital photos and keep notes of your observations.

Pro Tip

I've created a **Project Start-Up Workbook** which is a sample project packet and includes instruction and worksheets for each section of the packet.

Log in and download your FREE **Project Start-Up Workbook** today!
www.RemodelingProfessor.com/RYK20

Chapter 4

The Elevator Pitch

Nobody can effectively design or construct your dream kitchen if you cannot describe what you need and want. So logically, the first thing we'll work on is defining your planned kitchen project.

Make your project definition short and sweet, but very accurate. It should be complete enough to fully convey the scope of the project. To do this, I suggest writing an *Elevator Pitch* project description.

An *elevator pitch* is the name given to a short, carefully worded sales pitch that salespeople memorize in case they get a chance meeting with a prospect. Their pitch is complete enough to explain their product or service, but short enough to be spoken in the time the elevator takes between floors.

Your remodeling elevator pitch will be used each time you speak to potential designers, remodelers, and merchants the first time you tell them about your project. The pitch should give them a complete description of the proposed work and the main goals for the new kitchen in thirty to forty-five seconds.

Your first homework assignment is to craft the elevator pitch for your project.

Keep in mind while writing your elevator pitch, that you're looking for more than, "Remodel my kitchen." While that is technically accurate, it doesn't convey any useful information to the listener. You should include the key ideas or features that will make the uniqueness of your project understood, but without rambling. Things like, "Gut the current kitchen; open up the current dining room wall; install new wood flooring in both rooms, with all new cabinets and stone countertops; then and add an island with counter seating for four." A description of this nature really helps your listener grasp the scope of your remodel.

When writing the elevator pitch for your kitchen, think about the project and write a few lines that describe what you are looking for. The first benefit of this exercise is that you will actually learn a great deal about your project! Chances are you don't already know everything you'd like to accomplish, certainly not in any great detail. So this will help you to understand your own project more deeply.

Keep in mind that you are not required to "solve" the design or come up with the answers. You are simply setting the parameters that your hired professional will use to devise a creative new solution for you.

Later on, while identifying qualified designers and remodelers, and again while shopping for many of the materials you will use, you will find it necessary to give this information. So try to define what you wish to accomplish in clear, simple terms.

When you have written the first draft of your kitchen elevator pitch, save it in your project file. Print a copy and read it regularly. Edit it as your understanding of the job grows or if your scope changes while you work on the rest of the Project Packet. We often alter our initial impressions as we advance, so be sure to go back and overhaul your description if it becomes necessary!

Once your draft has taken shape, read it out loud in front of a mirror. Time it to make sure it is at least thirty seconds, but not much more than forty-five seconds.

The goal is to write and then memorize a concise, accurate description of your project. You will use it over and over as you meet prospective designers, remodelers, and product vendors, so give it your best effort.

Action Item #3:

Write the first draft of your project's Elevator Pitch **now**, before moving ahead to the next chapter.

Pro Tip

I've created a **Project Start-Up Workbook** which is a sample project packet and includes instruction and worksheets for each section of the packet.

Log in and download your FREE **Project Start-Up Workbook** today!
www.RemodelingProfessor.com/RYK20

Chapter 5

The Need List

The chewy caramel center of every remodeling project is the Need List. So let's discuss what a Need List is and how it relates to your kitchen.

For our purposes a NEED is an **indispensable item or feature** in the project you are planning. The Needs for your kitchen are so important that if they cannot be included, you will not perform the project. They are absolute *musts*.

Needs differ for every family, and for every project. Line up ten neighbors, all with similar houses of a similar age, all of whom are planning a kitchen remodel, and I guarantee that the Need List of every family will be different. There isn't one universal set of items and features that will make a kitchen universally successful for everyone. Each person, each couple, and each family have unique Needs when it comes to planning their kitchen remodels.

I want you to be aware that Needs and goals are not the same thing. *Needs* are specific items or features that either get included in the project or don't. In contrast, *goals* are what you want the results of the project to be. Your *goal* is to remodel and update the kitchen. Your *Need* might be an island, a 6-burner cooktop, or counter seating. So these terms are not interchangeable.

Taking this one step further, Needs are not things like stoves, refrigerators, or sinks. Those are essential elements that are required in every kitchen. Without those items the room would not be a kitchen. But your Need might be a specific material, type, or brand of range, fridge, or sink!

So Needs are the items and features that are a step above the obvious, and customize the room just for you.

For example, some people would call undercabinet lighting a need. Some would call a second oven a need. For some, it's counter seating, while for others it's a particular type of countertop material. Can you have a successful kitchen without these items and elements? Sure! But for owners who consider these features essential, they are elevated to Need status, and they go on their Need List.

Think about your project for a few minutes and ask yourself what are the absolutely essential elements that you cannot live without. Those are your core Needs. Don't worry about this list—you can't be wrong!

As you move further along in this book and you learn new information, you are very likely to modify your Need List, perhaps adding or deleting some items.

Now, if you have a spouse or partner, I suggest that you **both** contribute to the Need List. Only when you both agree to remove items should they be deleted. You could also make a note to whom a particular Need is attributed, so your designer can get additional input from that person to make the solution a perfect fit.

Need Lists are essential for every professionally designed or constructed kitchen. They are even more beneficial for larger, more involved projects. If you remodel without one, your architect or designer can only design a generic solution. Don't skimp here. When you spend the amount of money required to renovate a kitchen, you deserve a custom solution tailored just for you!

If your kitchen is part of a larger remodeling project (a multi-room renovation or addition, for example), you still require a Need List for your kitchen, but you should also make a separate Need List for each other room or area involved! Do this, because those other areas also have dozens of features and elements that qualify as Needs. (Some examples might be the TV location, types of window or skylight, fireplace, flooring type, views, planning for specific furniture, or maybe a built-in window seat.)

An adjacent mudroom might include Needs like a bench with built-in cubbies or storage for kids' shoes, clothes, jackets, and school items. You might also require extra storage, folding space, clothes-hanging space, an easy-clean floor, or a slop sink in a mudroom laundry area.

You should also consider any Needs for auxiliary spaces such as an adjacent patio, deck, or porch that will be constructed or modified along with your kitchen.

The bottom line is this: there are Needs. So the Need List is the most critical thing you can do to help your professionals really understand the unique custom nature of your new kitchen.

It's time to start writing out your Need List(s). Before moving ahead to the next chapter, write a draft of your kitchen Need List. If you have other rooms involved in your project, make those separate Need Lists, but store them all together for easy review and updating.

Remember, your Need List is a work in progress. Don't waste time or worry about each item. If you have any doubt if a function or feature is a Need for you – just include it on your list for now.

As you learn more, your Need List can be changed. I'm not suggesting you get talked out of your Needs! It's just that most homeowners think certain items are Needs, but they often learn about better options later on, or they determine that some features were not really essential.

Action Item #4:

Start your Need List now. Write out all the project Needs that you can identify, and describe any that are complex. Perhaps you can also find photos that illustrate your vision of the Need List items. Save or store these images in conjunction with your Need List.

Remember, you want other people to "see your vision." To do this properly, **you** must be clear about your Needs first. Only then can you clearly communicate them to the professionals helping you design and construct the solution.

Make a Need List for each adjacent or additional room being remodeled along with your kitchen. Store these Need Lists together in the same location.

Pro Tip:

I've created a **Project Start-Up Workbook** which is a sample project packet and includes instruction and worksheets for each section of the packet.

Log in and download your FREE **Project Start-Up Workbook** today!
www.RemodelingProfessor.com/RYK20

Chapter 6

The Wish List

If something isn't a Need, is it unimportant? No way! Just because a feature that you love is not "indispensable," it doesn't mean you don't want it!

In fact, most of the fun and exciting looks, brands, and features you really want in your new kitchen are NOT Needs! So where do these items get saved?

That's where the **WISH List** comes in. For our purposes, a Wish List item or feature is anything you really want but is not an indispensable Need.

Remember earlier when I said that you may initially declare things to be Needs, then maybe remove them from the Need List later? Well, the Wish List is where they go unless you choose to dismiss them and disregard them entirely.

The Wish List is full of items and features that you would really like to see in your solution, budget permitting. In the end, anything on this list might be omitted from the project because it didn't work well in the new layout, or because you changed your mind, or your budget ran out, making the feature unaffordable.

Remember, the distinction between a Need and a Wish is the fact that Needs are indispensable (without them the project will not happen), while Wish List items are desired and valued, but they only make it into the project if the budget allows.

For example, wishes *might* be things like a bay or bow window, a cabinet-style pantry, a built-in for cookbooks and recipes, a decorative range hood, or a premium glass tile backsplash (or many, many others).

These features would make you very happy and the kitchen even nicer. But in order to be included in the final design, each Wish List item has to be individually worked into the solution by a talented architect or kitchen designer, and there needs to be a sufficient budget to pay for them.

Action Item #5:

Go write your first Wish List now. List and describe the items and features you'd like to work into your new kitchen design—budget permitting. Do this without worrying about the order you list them or their potential cost.

Once you have written out a draft of your Wish List, begin to prioritize it. By this I mean organizing the list so that the items and features you want most are on top of the list. Then, continue to rank the rest of the Wish List items you listed using those same priorities.

You may find that items and features on the Wish List get promoted to the Need List, move up or down the Wish List, or get eliminated based on your changing priorities as the project goes along. It is not uncommon that items become more or less important as you investigate them and learn more about different alternatives. Occasionally, you'll find a new feature that you were unaware of at the beginning, that can replace an original Need List item or a highly ranked Wish List item. That's perfectly okay.

In the end, this is a great way to help your design professional understand your thinking about what specialty features and items should be most highly considered in your ideal kitchen. As you move forward in the process, constantly review and update your Need and Wish Lists, keeping them as accurate as possible.

Another note about how the Wish List gets used is this: the quality of your architect or designer makes a **huge difference** in the number of Wish List features that get included! Truly talented designers often find creative ways to cost-effectively combine elements, allowing more Wish List items to become part of the solution. So when it comes to which design pro you use, select someone very skilled and creative, but excellent at designing to a budget.

Finally, I think everyone needs to understand the approximate cost of their Wish List items. Here's why: if the designer comes in $3,000 below your target budget—then you can still afford to add some Wish List items. But which one or ones? If your first item is a $2,800 feature and the next three or four after that total just $2,500, would you still get the first item only? Or would you add the next three or four features instead?

It goes without saying that at some point the relative price on one item as opposed to three or four other items would surely make a difference to many owners. So once you prioritize your Wish List, try to determine the approximate cost of the highest-ranked items and features so that you are prepared to make value choices if it comes down to the last few dollars.

Action Item #6:

Go reread your Wish List first draft. Confirm that you would still like to have all the items and features you listed earlier (budget permitting). Then make any additions or deletions you consider necessary.

Then prioritize your Wish List items in the order you want them added to the project.

Finally, research the top few Wish List items so you are aware of their approximate costs and can make decisions between them more easily if the need arises.

Remember, you should revisit and update the Wish List and the priority order often.

Pro Tip

I've created a **Project Start-Up Workbook** which is a sample project packet and includes instruction and worksheets for each section of the packet.

Log in and download your FREE **Project Start-Up Workbook** today!
www.RemodelingProfessor.com/RYK20

Chapter 7

The Budget

After creating an Elevator Pitch description and writing out Need and Wish Lists for your kitchen, it's time to talk about what you'll pay to accomplish the work.

Remember, just like the Boss in the plush corner office—you're following those same steps as you get ready to advertise and interview prospective new employees. And a huge part of the process is determining what you're willing to pay your new employee.

But how do you do that? You have no idea what kitchen remodeling projects actually cost, right? So how can you set a proper budget?

First, let me define some important terminology. Cost and budget are not identical. **Cost** is the price charged to the homeowner by the remodeling contractor. It is a combination of the material prices, the labor price, and the profit and overhead (or markup) of a remodeling company. I understand that you can't possibly know the real cost of your project until you obtain it directly from a remodeler. And since we are only beginning to prepare for the process, we will not be doing that. So, for the time being, we'll set aside the idea of the project cost and look at a remodeling budget.

The **Budget** is the pile of money from which you pay for all your remodeling-related expenses. This may include design costs and remodeling costs.

So, while the actual cost is determined by the remodelers, the budget for any project is always set by you, the homeowner. And you do that now, well in advance of even meeting with remodeling candidates.

Here is the logic to apply as you set your remodeling budget:

You only have a certain amount of money available to use for the project. Some may be savings, perhaps some is from investments, and maybe you'll tap your home equity. If those totals are low, you might be in a position to consider home improvement loans. Regardless of how you obtain the funds, there is a finite amount that you will be **able to spend**.

But how much of the money that you are able to spend are you also **willing to spend**? It's often not wise to spend more than you are comfortable parting with, or easily able to repay (in the case of loans).

So I suggest that your maximum budget is quite simply the **amount you are both able *and* willing to spend**.

To state it another way—you are able and willing to pay your budgeted amount in exchange for accomplishing everything on your Need List.

Before you settle on a final budget figure, there are still a couple factors to consider. These may affect what you're able to spend, or what you're willing to spend.

Loans

Many homeowners borrow money to pay for larger remodeling projects, including kitchens.   NOTE: if you will not borrow money for your kitchen remodel, you can skip ahead to the next discussion about Current Home Value.

Let me be clear, I am not a loan specialist or a financial advisor. When it comes time to get details about loans you may need for your project, you'll do that with trained people that can give you all the details of their particular loans.

But as your personal industry insider, I want to help you avoid higher costs. In this case, that means avoiding one particular type of loan.

In the eyes of your remodeling contractor, there are only two types of payments: payments that are made by the homeowner (you), or payments that are made by the bank. That's it. The type of loan you obtain will affect whether you write the checks or the bank writes the checks. It's important that you understand this point.

Every remodeler prefers to be paid immediately after handing the homeowner an invoice. That only happens when the homeowner writes the checks. When the bank writes the checks, the remodeler typically has to wait and additional two to four weeks to get a check from the bank. This is why remodelers consider bank-controlled loans to be a major hassle and why they typically increase their price to you by 5 or 10 percent to compensate for the annoying delays in getting paid.

So whenever possible, obtain loans that allow you to issue the payments. This lets you negotiate a more favorable total price.

Another important piece of loan advice is to **visit your bank/lender LONG BEFORE you ever interview remodelers**. It takes a month or two for most loans to be approved and another few weeks for the paperwork and funding to be completed. So visit your lender well in advance. Additionally, you'll already know your loan limit, your rate, and your approximate payments BEFORE you set your budget.

Finally, being prequalified, you can sign a contract without frustrating or annoying your remodeler with a 45 to 120-day delay while the loan is processed. Yes, it really does take that long to finalize many loans. Please don't wait.

Action Item #7:

All loans take time to arrange. Start loan shopping early in the process to find out what limitations you may have that could affect your loan type, maximum amount, or loan rate and payments, or the amount of time it takes to approve and fund your loan. This is important information to help you set the budget, but it is also important in the eyes of your remodeler since it affects how they get paid.

Do this before you interview remodelers so that you and they both know the payment situation in advance of writing the proposal and signing the contract.

There is another loan type worthy of mention, and that is a signature loan. The most common form of signature loan is a credit card. The lender offers you money based only on your signature and your ability to repay.

As you know, these loans have fairly low borrowing limits and very high-interest rates, so they are *not* an ideal way to fund remodeling projects.

But when you remodel a kitchen, using your credit card can be very beneficial if you use it wisely. I discuss the creative use of credit cards in the section on Saving Money later in the book.

Your Current Home Value

As you're setting a budget for your planned kitchen remodel, you might consider the current value of your home. Let's look a few reasons for this.

It's good to understand the current value of your home relative to other top homes in your area. Knowing the value of your home also helps you verify how much equity is in it.

Most kitchen remodels are not so expensive that they will push the value of your home past the top home values in your neighborhood. In fact, most kitchen renovations will bring a sub-par or outdated kitchen back up to current standards or just above those. Sure, your home's value rises with a professionally performed kitchen remodel. But the increase is not huge unless your project is very high end or is part of a larger remodeling project.

If you're planning a larger project along with the kitchen, you are more likely to consider a bank loan due to the larger total cost. When you apply for these loans, your home will be appraised as part of the loan process. This is the most accurate way to establish its value short of selling it on the open market.

While there are many other ways to "kind of" work out your home's current value (from realtors, appraisal websites, tax values, watching sales of comparable homes nearby, etc.), the easiest and best way is to pay for a home appraisal. To hire an appraiser, you might pay between $400 and $600, but you can be sure the home value is reasonably accurate.

Don't trust appraisal websites that give "estimates" or display home values (like Zillow and Homesnap). Use those only for general information, not precise values.

Cost versus Value

I already explained how to set your baseline remodeling budget. It is the amount you are able and willing to spend to accomplish your Need List.

Most homeowners have two big questions at this point when I teach this material, and I suspect you are asking them too.

- How do I set a realistic budget without knowing anything about the true **cost** of kitchen remodeling projects?
- **How much value** do the different levels of kitchen remodeling add to the home's value when they are completed?

These are both very reasonable questions. Let's look at these two topics one at a time.

Cost

I believe it's important to have an idea of what real-life projects cost. I've seen too many shocked faces when I give real-world estimates to homeowners.

Besides, if a budget is truly inadequate for the scope of work desired, you want to know immediately... before investing too much time, effort, and money.

So where can you get honest and accurate information about the cost of typical remodeling projects? Well, the first step is NOT to ask Google or Bing. You will get an endless variety of prices that are ambiguous, with price ranges far too large to be useful. Most online costs are opinions at best, and they are not very realistic.

You also cannot learn about cost and value by watching HGTV remodeling shows. As enjoyable as many HGTV shows are, they are purely entertainment. While they appear to be reality TV, they are quite unrealistic about the actual costs, the full scope of work, and the construction timeframes. Everything in real life costs more and takes longer than what you've seen on TV. Please… feel free to get inspired by watching TV remodeling shows, but don't fall into the trap that what you are seeing is "real," or you'll be very disappointed.

So, where can you turn?

There is one outstanding source for accurate remodeling cost figures. It happens to be an insider source for the remodeling industry. It is an annual report called the **Cost vs. Value Report** (CVVR). The name says it all. It provides answers to both our questions—realistic costs of common projects and how much value is added by those same projects.

You can find the most recent report by typing "cost versus value report" into your search engine. Then click on the current/newest year report link in the list. The names associated with the original report are *Remodeling Magazine* and/or *the Journal of Light Construction.*

When you get to the page, you will see the latest Cost vs. Value Report article. While you're there, feel free to read the article about how costs of projects and their values have changed nationwide over the past year. This is always interesting, but the best information lies in the localized reports.

To access the localized report, you should select the proper region of the country and then click on the closest city to you within your region. I suggest downloading the PDF report so you can read or print it as desired.

The Cost versus Value Report obtains project information from realtors and remodeling experts in every region and city listed. These professionals establish the costs and values that the report describes. As a result, you get very localized information on different project costs and values for your area. And there is a new report every year!

The report includes prices and values for *several types of kitchen projects*. The details of the midrange and the upscale kitchens are very carefully described. One of those two is likely to be closer to the scope of work you are considering. Be sure to look very carefully at their descriptions to learn how their kitchen and your kitchen are similar and how they differ. Then you can mentally adjust their cost figure based on those differences to arrive at your kitchen's cost and value.

This resource provides you with an excellent starting place for accurate job costs. If you guessed that your job might cost $30,000, you will probably have sticker shock when you see the CVVR midrange kitchen cost listed just above $50,000. But now you have a trustworthy number.

Because remodeling costs are shocking, I believe it's better to know the real cost at the beginning so you go through the process with your eyes open. The worst way to learn about real-world prices is to spend a few months working with remodelers and find out things are unaffordable when you're presented with a final proposal or a contract to sign. Finding out that your price expectation was wrong that late in the process can be devastating (not to mention costly).

So don't glance at the first kitchen price you see listed in the report and take that figure at face value. If you know that you will select more upscale items or perform a larger project, your price will be higher than the one listed. To the extent that you plan to use more economical items or keep your project smaller than their description, your cost will be lower. If you are careful in comparing your project and theirs, these reports provide an excellent way to obtain realistic working prices (and values) for your project.

After this, you will be able to talk to lenders (if necessary) and then set your project budget with much more confidence.

Value

Just how much value is added when remodeling your kitchen? We turn again to the Cost vs. Value Report, and this time we'll focus on the VALUE listings.

The report asks the hypothetical question, "If you spend the estimated price on the project described and you sell the home right after it is complete, how much will the project raise the home's selling price?" That is the basis for the value figures reported.

Remember, in a home that has not been fully maintained and updated over time, the value added by remodeling might only bring that home back on par with other well-maintained neighborhood homes. This fact is not built into the CVV Report, but you need to take it into account for your home.

Generally, a major kitchen renovation adds about 60 to 70 percent of its cost to the current value of the home.

There's another added "value" that homeowners seldom recognize which is very important. As you live in your remodeled home, you enjoy the improved function and utility of the home on a daily basis. When you spread that great feeling over four, six, or even ten years, that project has actually paid off handsomely.

If the planning and interview portions of your remodeling project go on for a while, revisit the Cost vs. Value Report when it is updated to learn how the costs and values may have changed since you started.

My goal for each project I design is that my client will say, "Wow! I sure am glad we did this project!" every single day. In well-crafted projects, that's the big payoff you get. That's the other twenty, thirty, or forty percent of your investment.

Moving Soon?

If you plan to move in three to five years, you should make **all** your remodeling decisions with an eye on resale. This does not necessarily mean that you should avoid all kitchen remodeling; just don't make it extravagant or personal. Stick to simpler solutions with neutral color palettes and traditional looks for your kitchen choices. You'll still get several years of enjoyment of the new kitchen, plus the benefit of selling the house with the term "newly remodeled" in the listing.

Pro Tip:

You may not realize this, but high-quality remodeling projects remain fresh and "recently remodeled" for as many as ten years after completion!

If you know that you will be moving in less than three years, you should stick with remedial or cosmetic improvements only and skip major kitchen remodeling with its high price tags and low payback values. Instead, repair and revive things in the kitchen without going all in. Focus instead on cosmetic projects that have eye appeal and which yield larger returns on investment.

If you're in this situation, consider painting, installing new light fixtures, updating tile, new and updated appliances, and possibly getting new flooring or refinishing the current wood floor. If the current cabinets **are not** in good condition, don't put lipstick on a pig. Skip the stone tops, new flooring, and tile backsplashes since the next buyer will tear it all out soon anyway.

Action Item #8

Set your kitchen budget.

Most often your budget is the amount that you are able **and** willing to spend to accomplish your Need List items. It can be affected by things like real-world project costs and value added by the project, the value of similar homes in your neighborhood, localized sale trends and values, how long you plan to remain in the home, and more.

You will want your design professional and your remodelers to know and understand this figure, especially if it is at the low end of the price spectrum for kitchens.

Pro Tip

I've created a **Project Start-Up Workbook** which is a sample project packet and includes instruction and worksheets for each section of the packet.

Log in and download your FREE **Project Start-Up Workbook** today!
www.RemodelingProfessor.com/RYK20

Chapter 8

Defining Your Project

So far in your **Project Packet**, you have worked on an Elevator Pitch, your Need and Wish Lists, and your Budget. Now it's time to get busy with some project-specific details. This organization and record keeping method helps you avoid becoming overwhelmed with the huge amount of detail that every remodeling project includes.

Before we start, however, this warning: don't worry! A professional will design your nifty new 3-D kitchen solution. **It's not your job or your responsibility to come up with the design for your kitchen!** Leave the design to the professionals. They live to solve tough problems like that.

Instead, in this chapter, you will learn how to record and organize all the details and choices for your project (whether on paper or in a computer spreadsheet). The first step is an inspired brainstorming session that lets you initially jot down many of the key ingredients for your ideal new kitchen. After that I'll explain the easiest way to organize those details so they can be easily reviewed, updated, and shared as you move through the remodeling process.

But first some basics. In this case a few thinking assignments for the new room.

A Few Introductory Thoughts

Here are a few unique factors to consider as you start defining your new room. Some of these ideas will inspire you to modify your Need or Wish Lists, or to create a separate page called "Other Factors" that can be added to your Project Packet for your architect or contractor.

These factors will either be totally applicable to your project or of no consequence to you. That's okay. You decide if you will pass any of this information on to your remodeling professionals.

- **Your FURNISHINGS drive the size and the layout of most rooms.** In your kitchen, the eating area (table or counter), the cabinets, and the appliances are the furniture. Furniture requires open space to function properly, and also enough space to move freely past it!
- **Would you look at that!** What is the FOCAL POINT of your kitchen? Is it the sink and window with a view? Is it a large island with counter seating? Perhaps a fabulous gas range and cooking center with a tile backsplash and decorative exhaust hood? You choose what you want visitors to notice and remember. You should plan your focal point and not just let it happen. Write it down to share with your designer.
- **Get a load of that VIEW!** Does your kitchen enjoy an excellent view to the yard? Will you orient the work spaces and seating to take advantage of that view? You can if you make plans right from the start! Perhaps the best kitchen connection is to an adjacent area like the Family Room. If so, consider those views too!
- **What do you LIKE?** Sometimes it's that simple. If you've seen or used various features that have worked for you before, then incorporate those into your new kitchen. Be sure to add these features to your lists!
- **What DON'T you like?** If you've had it and hated it, don't do it again. If something doesn't work for you, be sure to avoid it this time. It seems to go without saying, but... if you don't like it, don't include it!

Each refinement you make to your vision of the new kitchen results in a higher-quality, customized solution!

Now it's time to talk about capturing and organizing the details and selections that define your project...

Functions and Features

The very first time I meet with any new client, I guide them through their imaginary project to get an idea of what they "see." I ask leading questions so I am sure that they have considered all aspects of their new kitchen. Each kitchen has a load of unique functions and features that need to be listed and then tracked, modified, and ultimately communicated to your chosen professionals.

To get you started, I'll ask some stimulating questions while you visualize your NEW kitchen. This exercise is ONLY about listing the new functions and features that you might like in your new kitchen. That's it! You just list and then organize this information for inclusion in your Project Packet.

If your project includes other rooms or areas, you will do this for each room or area individually. That's because each room has a very different set of functions and features. As an architect, I found this type of input invaluable in helping me understand clients' needs so I could customize their solution accordingly.

Two simple terms hold the key to understanding and defining any room. Understanding these will help you to imagine and organize your new kitchen. These terms define everything that happens in your kitchen: Functions & Features.

Functions

Every kitchen has food preparation as its primary function. But there are many additional functions performed in those kitchens too. Cleaning, for example!

We all clean using products and items stored in our kitchens. Nearly every kitchen also has some form of eating take place, but how that is accomplished varies drastically. Do you eat at a table with chairs, or on stools at an island or peninsula? If you have young kids, it's likely that some homework will be performed in the kitchen. We also store cookbooks and recipes there... maybe coupons and shopping lists too. And everyone has a proverbial "junk drawer" that stores all those important non-kitcheny things!

You might need to watch the kids play in the back yard while you're in the kitchen. Maybe you'll want to see and converse with people in adjacent rooms and areas? Surely some type of arts and crafts will also happen in the kitchen. I imagine that you will also entertain in the kitchen. Perhaps you will play family games there? Maybe you'll read? Answer and write emails? Pay bills? Only you know for sure!

A very important and fairly new Function often found in today's kitchens is the storage of mail/purses/cell phones/tablets along with the charging of our many electric devices. I call this location a "drop spot" and try to plan one based on the specific needs of each family.

Clearly, you now realize the wide variety of **functions** that can take place in a kitchen. Which ones will happen in your newly remodeled space?

Write down **all the FUNCTIONS** you envision happening in your kitchen.

Features

In nearly every kitchen, you will find a sink, a dishwasher, a refrigerator, and an appliance or two on which to cook. But do you choose to cook on a range or a cooktop? Gas or electric? Do you require a full-time second oven? What about a microwave? Do you want stacked wall ovens? How is your cooking surface exhausted? Up through a hood and out the roof? Through an exterior wall vent? Or down through a cabinet and into the floor? Is your sink a double-bowl or single-bowl style? Is it stainless steel or another material? Is it located on the island, or by a window? Is there a second sink in the kitchen? Will you have a separate refrigerator and freezer? Will you have a spare refrigerator? An ice maker?

Will your countertop be tile? Stone? Laminate? Butcher block? Or something exotic like concrete or bamboo? Will you have a tile backsplash? Perhaps a granite splash? Or painted drywall?

What about your floor material? Sheet vinyl, hardwood, bamboo, cork, and tile are all commonly found on today's kitchen floors.

How about specialty appliances like a super mixer, blender, waffle iron, bread machine, coffee machine, or toaster oven? Will they live inside your cabinets, in closets, or on the counter?

Where will you store your dry food? In cabinets or a pantry closet? Will you need to keep a step stool or a broom and dustpan handy? What about those occasional items like the turkey platter, deviled egg plate, and cake transporter? Where will those be stored?

Then there are the cabinets. Are you in love with one particular door style? Maybe a specific wood and stain combination? Maybe a painted cabinet? Are there special cabinetry features that you absolutely need to have?

Write down **every key FEATURE** you anticipate in your remodeled kitchen.

Perhaps, as I listed all these functions and features, you began to understand that the simple room labels we use don't even come close to describing all that goes on inside the room. This is why architects and other professional designers don't rely on room names alone when designing solutions for clients. They require lots of personal input in order to create a custom solution that responds to the unique requirements of each unique family.

A kitchen is **not** just a kitchen. A specific list of **functions and features** allows your design professional to craft a custom solution to meet your specific needs.

Homeowners are not trained to think about or visualize rooms the way architects view or describe them. But your understanding of your project will grow a great deal as you work on this exercise. You'll become aware of many ideas you never knew were a thing. And you'll become increasingly more observant.

For now, there's no right or wrong, no judgment, and no consideration of cost or value—just a thumbs up or thumbs down about whether you might like a given function or feature in your ideal kitchen. Later on in the process you might choose to edit these details or remove some items altogether.

While you do this exercise, you may find that you need to record additional information about some features. Go ahead and add those notes after you list the feature. For example, your refrigerator might need to be a french-door style with bottom freezer. Or your cooktop might be a six-burner gas model with a matching hood. Go ahead and add those clarifying notes behind the name of that feature. Every little bit of information helps.

Bear in mind that **you do not need to make every decision here and now**. Later on, in "Section 5: Through My Eyes", I go into much more detail about planning the space needs of your kitchen, and the best order in which to make your major decisions.

For now, if you don't know which countertop material you want, create a line for "countertop" and list the options you're considering, then make your final choice later. Or write down "flooring—wood or ceramic tile," and edit the entry when you make up your mind down the line. Don't think too hard, and don't worry. Just brainstorm and write this stuff down. We'll organize all your Features and descriptive notes later!

Organizing Your Information

After reading about some of the Functions and Features of typical kitchens, you are starting to realize that even modest kitchen remodels have many, many details. To coordinate and organize all your information, I suggest a that you use a simple table (or a spreadsheet if you prefer working digitally).

Tables are an excellent way to coordinate the many details for each remodeled room or area. Your table serves as the single collection point for all the choices and selections you make about your kitchen going forward.

Whether you use graph paper and a pencil or a computer spreadsheet to record your area-by-area descriptions makes no difference as you start planning.

If your kitchen is part of an addition, or if you are combining the kitchen with an adjacent dining or family room, then create a separate table for each room or area. Just be sure to put all your kitchen details on a single table.

Make something like the following sample table as you set yours up. The table below uses a simple two-column format that I recommend as you start coordinating your project details.

KITCHEN SELECTION TABLE & Notes

FUNCTIONS: Cooking, food storage, dry good storage, small appliance storage, eating for 5+, views to yard, open to DR & FR
NEED LIST: Open wall to DR & FR, painted cabinets w/ granite tops and undermount sink, LED lighting w/ dimmers in Decora style,
New double window at sink (sliding), tile backsplash. Island with counter-seating for 5. MW vents to exterior. Focal Point = Island

	FEATURE	NOTES AND COMMENTS (as needed for clarity)
CEILING	Drywall Ceiling, smooth, painted	Paint Color = Ceiling flat white
	Recessed lights at work areas	LED flood bulbs. 150W equivalent (dimmable).
	Ceiling mounted lights (3) over island	LED bulbs. Customer supplied, installed by remodeler.
WALLS	Drywall, smooth, painted	Color unknown at this time
	Tile backsplash - tops to upper cabs and over range	Tile purchased and supplied by Owner, installed by remodeler.
FLOOR	Oak flooring (match flooring in DR)	Continue DR/FR floor throughout kitchen
CONTENTS	Cabinets	Painted, Shaker style door, Full Overlay. Brand, material, color not yet selected.
	Cabinetry knobs & pulls	Owner supplied - remodeler installed
	Countertop	Granite. Color not selected yet.
	RANGE	36" gas + electric, 5 burner
	MICROWAVE	NOT ON COUNTER. Maybe over range, maybe built-in. Vented to outside.
	REFRIGERATOR / FREEZER	36" French Doors, bottom freezer. Brand/model not yet selected. "Built into" a wall.
	DISHWASHER	BOSCH stainless steel unit, 24", model not yet selected
	ISLAND Notes	STORAGE ONLY (no appliances). Seating for 5+ around corner or curve (not all in a row).
	Pantry Cabinets	Same brand/style as main cabinets. 2 30-36" roll-out trayunits flanking REF.

As seen in the sample table, I prefer to place a unique room name at the top of my tables for easy identification. Then I list all the **FUNCTIONS** that will take place in that room to keep them in mind as decisions are made. This is also very handy for your architect or kitchen designer when they get involved.

Below the FUNCTIONS is a simple two-column table. The main column contains the name of each Feature found in that room. The column to the right contains any notes or details about the feature on that line (if any are known at this time). One Feature goes on each line of the table.

Left of the two main columns I add the room location for each feature. The sample table shows how I organize **Features** from the top down (Ceiling first, then Walls, Floors, and finally Contents). I find that arranging the details this way on all my room tables makes it far easier to locate information since they are all laid out the same way.

In most rooms the "contents" of the room are the furniture you plan to use. But kitchen furniture is typically limited to a table and chairs (or stools). Go ahead and list those if you plan to use them. However, when I design kitchens, I also list the cabinets, countertops, appliances, and plumbing fixtures as "contents". So this section of the table collects any items that are not an integral part of the ceiling, walls, or floor of the room.

Pro Tip:

In my room tables I use room location descriptions (Ceiling, Walls, Floor, or Contents) to arrange my Features. This logical organization lets me start listing features at the top of each room and work my way down the walls to the floor. Then I list the unique contents for that particular room or area.

This makes finding specific items in any room table a lot easier (to add or update information, or when reviewing the table).

When you do list furniture on a room table, use a separate line for each unique piece, and try to list the dimensions. Do this for the furniture you own, and estimate the size of furniture you plan to buy. This helps your design professional reserve enough space for your furniture, or lets them quickly determine whether it all will fit.

To review, the main two columns are for your FEATURES and any current NOTES about those features.

So, to get started, think about the kitchen from the top down. Do a mental inventory of your planned kitchen and list ALL the Features you can think of in the left-hand column.

Then start back at the top of the table in the right-hand column and list any notes or comments that relate to each feature you listed to the left. Write down information or attributes of your features, such as size, color, style, brand, material, or any other details that help you (or your designer) understand each feature fully. This is a very simple method to capture and organize a great deal of information quickly, so you can refer back to it easily.

After you have a first draft of the room table for your new Kitchen, it becomes your one-stop source for all the details about your project.

Any time you change your mind about a feature or note listed in your tables (and you *will* change your mind), just edit your table! If you decide not to use butcher block (wood) countertops in the kitchen, but you want to use granite instead, just replace the old entry with your new countertop material. If you settle on a particular granite color, add that information in the note also.

As you become aware of additional Features you need to select, or which need to be communicated to your architect or kitchen designer, just add a new row for those Features to keep your table current.

This is a simple and effective way to keep all your choices and selections in one place. Homeowners routinely become overwhelmed by the number of choices and decisions—especially in kitchens. Tables let you organize your choices. They also show you at a glance which decisions you have already made and which decisions still need to be made.

Pro Tip:

Don't get overwhelmed by the number of selections, choices, and details in your kitchen. Do one thing at a time, and it will take as long as it takes.

When you make a decision, move on to the next task or item. Still unsure about a selection? Highlight it! This makes it easy to revisit later. Then move on to the next choice or decision.

Whatever your rooms call for in terms of Features, give each one a unique line, and fill in what you know about it at this moment. If you know that more information or a final decision will be coming soon, just list the feature name and leave the notes blank as a placeholder.

Now let's talk about two final table organizing ideas I want to share with you. I'll cover each one briefly.

First, you have already listed your room Features from the top of the room down (ceiling-related features, then wall features, then floor features, and finally the room contents). Every now and then you may have something that doesn't fit neatly into one of those categories. If that happens to you, list those oddball features LAST (below the room Contents). If you do this the same way every time on every table, you'll always be able to find them.

Second, you will occasionally need multiple lines of information for the same Feature (material). For instance, some rooms have more than one color of wall paint. Some tile work includes stripes, borders, edges, or other decorative pieces in addition to the field tile. Also, with tile, you might mix more than one style in your floor or backsplash. When this happens, make MULTIPLE lines for paint, or MULTIPLE lines for tile (or whatever your duplicated Feature is), and on each line give the unique information that separates that specific material from the rest (model, color, size, material, etc.). This keeps all the "same" materials together on your table so that when you shop or place orders, the information is all in one convenient place.

Action Item #9:

Make a draft of your table now. If other adjacent rooms or areas in your project are also Involved, do a separate table for each room. Set it up with the room name on top. List all the key Functions that will take place in your room right below the room title.

Organize Features from the top of the room down (Ceiling, Walls, Floor, Contents).

The first (left) column lists each Feature you need to select or choose for your kitchen. Give every Feature (material or item) a row of its own (as in the sample table).

In the second (right) column of your table, write any comments or notes you have regarding each Feature listed.

Take your time. Work on it regularly for a week and add new Features that come to mind. If you come up with more details or information about existing Features, add those too. Update the Features and their notes each time you review the table.

Be sure to create rows for future Features that you know are still coming (light fixtures, faucets, countertops, etc.) and use them as placeholders (reminders that you will need to investigate and make a selection in the future). HINT: if you make a table on paper, leave room to the right for future columns!

I also suggest highlighting all rows with missing information to visually remind you of what still needs doing. This helps you see the difference between already chosen items and unmade selections with just a glance.

Supercharging Your Tables

At this point, your Kitchen table is a basic two-column table that shows the Features and the corresponding notes and information you are currently aware of.

Now I will help you supercharge your table so you can fully organize all the information you will collect during your remodeling journey. We will also make some improvements that let your team see the critical details while they design and as they start placing orders on your behalf.

Your Needs

My first suggestion is very simple and will make sense immediately.

Write your kitchen NEED LIST Items (the indispensable items or features that must be included in the solution) under the Room Name at the top of your table.

Your sheet will now show the title KITCHEN. Then on the next line appears the list of your kitchen Need List items. The following line still lists the FUNCTIONS that will take place in the kitchen, and your table still starts below this information.

Keeping the NEEDS and FUNCTIONS featured at the top of your table with all the known or anticipated FEATURES in the table puts the motherlode of information together in one spot and helps your architect or kitchen designer and your remodeler deliver a more precise and accurate solution.

Help them to help you.

Additional Information

My second suggestion is to **expand** your table. Add new columns to the right of the Feature column (the first major column on the left). Add as many or as few as you need based on the Features in your table and the amount of information each new column holds.

Additional column titles that I have used before include: Brand, Model #, Color, Cost, Style/Type, Material, and URL. If you have such a piece of information for several different Features on your table, it might help to add a column for that topic (leaving it empty if a particular feature doesn't use that information).

Now you can collect all kinds of information in your table. It will become the go-to location for everything you need to know about any Feature (item or material) in your project.

When you keep a digital spreadsheet on the computer, you can include information like web addresses (URLs) of the product's manufacturer, links to photographs of the items (yours or retail versions), sites where you found the item(s) for sale, typical prices, and much, much more.

Adding this type of extra information about the Features you will use for your project is what makes this table so incredibly valuable to you and to your design and remodeling team.

Why You Do It

The entire Project Packet eliminates critical and costly mistakes that homeowners make all the time.

This specific exercise, creating your Kitchen table (pun intended), will help you stay sane, avoid detail overwhelm, and keep you supremely organized throughout your remodeling journey.

Having all your project details saved in a simple, carefully organized table that remains up to date is groundbreaking. It's easy to organize and is easily referenced and shared whenever you need it.

As you progress through your project, you will learn more about various options and materials, and some of your early preferences and decisions will change. Your opinions about some materials will be revised as you work with your design and remodeling pros. Simply revisit your table to update those selections and choices. This is especially easy on a computer spreadsheet.

I urge you to look at your Table often as you go forward in the process (at least weekly for now) to keep this critical information in your mind and in front of your eyes. As you make more decisions and move further into the process, your reviews will happen a bit less often.

Your designer and remodeler will give you deadlines for final selections of different materials, letting you know which items to focus on first. For instance, flooring and cabinet decisions need to be completed far earlier than countertop decisions and paint colors. The architect needs appliance types in order to lay out your solution, while the style of drawer pulls to be used is a last-minute choice.

So as you get going, fill in what you know (or think you want), and every time you go through the table, update things until you have a complete list of Features and good support information for each one.

Obviously you will have to "shop" for many items to learn what your various options are and which ones are best for you. But doing a little bit at a time and starting months before the information is required lets you explore more, learn more, and choose a better set of materials (Features) based on your particular style and budget.

Keep your Lists and Table current because you improve the quality of your final solution with each tweak and revision. You deserve a personally customized kitchen solution!

Action Item #10:

Expand your table with new columns now.

Start by listing the Need List items for your kitchen right below the Room Name and above the key Functions that take place in your new kitchen.

Then expand your table by adding a few new columns for things like the brand, model number, size, color or finish, or other data that is important. KEEP the Notes column for customized and unique details. You can also link images or manufacturer URLs there. This makes your table your one-stop source for all project selection information!

Then get in the habit of reviewing and updating your table regularly. Update the list of Features (editing them as they change) and keep the specific information you know about them current. Review your early assumptions about Features and materials, and replace those that have changed or been eliminated.

Maintain the table as well as possible, reviewing it weekly until you have completed the majority of your selections or turned them all over to your pros.

Remember how vitally important this task is. However, recognize that you have a good deal of time to complete it while you move forward in the process. Your professionals will be able to give you a significantly better design and a customized finished product if you are able to share a complete table with them.

Pro Tip:

Your **Project Packet** sets your vision for the new kitchen. The more fully your professionals understand that vision, the better your solution will be.

I've created a Project Packet Template which includes a sample Kitchen table you can refer to while you create your table!

Log in and download your FREE Kitchen **Project Packet** template today!

www.RemodelingProfessor.com/RYK20

Chapter 9

Final Touches

The definitions, notes, lists, and tables you have produced so far will help you keep track of your project's details, and they'll help your design professionals create a successful custom kitchen solution for you.

But before you contact a design professional or a contractor about your project, there are a few more pieces of information to track down and add to the back of your Project Packet. These can be digital scans, copies, or prints.

- **Plot Plan** – In most jurisdictions, remodeling projects that require a building permit need a plot plan as part of the permit submission packet. They are also known as *house location surveys*. Your architect or remodeling contractor will take the current copy you provide and show the permitting authority the new work location and size. The title company usually includes a copy of your house location survey in the documents you receive when you settle on your home. If you can't find one, many surveyors will create one for between $250 and $500. Realtors often know of local surveyors that can provide realty-quality plot plans at reasonable prices. Occasionally, your architect or remodeler can get enough data online to create one also—so be sure to ask.
- **HOA/Architectural Committee Forms** – If your home is part of an HOA or your community has an architectural committee, you may need to submit information to them for approval. Verify whether your project will require a hearing. If so, obtain the required forms that your architect or remodeler can help you fill out before you apply for approval. Add copies of those forms to your Packet.

- **Appliance cut sheets** (for all sizes/dimensions/specs of your items). These manufacturer sheets tell the cabinet folks, plumber, and electrician all the exact measurements and details they need in order to do their job and set the kitchen up to accept your new appliances. You can usually get PDF copies free online or printed copies from the appliance distributor.
- **Manufacturer specification sheets** for your major material selections (appliances, most flooring types, and cabinetry falls into this category). You may also find these sheets for your lighting fixtures and some other selected items.
- **List of all known current house materials.** You only need this information if you are keeping the existing materials and using them in the new solution (like a particular brand or type of flooring, siding, window, etc., that you want to match in the newly remodeled room).

Action Item #11:

Add any Final Touches listed above to your Project Packet now:
  * Add known URLs and image links into your table now.
  * Add your Plot Plan and other Finishing Touches to your Packet.

Don't make the creation of your Project Packet more difficult than it should be. Make one choice or one decision at a time. Then move on to the next choice or decision, and keep doing that.

Maintain that attitude as you work on your Project Packet and you'll simplify the most critical task in the remodeling process (one that most people are not even aware they should do!). This task makes the difference between an "okay" result, and a working custom kitchen!

So, keep your Lists and Table current because you improve the quality of your final solution with each tweak and revision.

Pro Tip

I've created a **Project Packet Template** which includes a sample Kitchen table you can refer to while you create your table!

Log in and download your FREE Kitchen **Project Packet** template today!
www.RemodelingProfessor.com/RYK20

Chapter 10

Assemble Your Project Packet

You've done the work to create a Project Packet. Now it's time to assemble it.

Print out your Project Packet parts:
- Elevator Pitch Description of your project
- Need List
- Wish List
- Budget
- Kitchen Selections & Materials Table
- Finishing Touches

The Project Packet can be printed or digital. The advantage of a digital Packet is that you and your team can access the information anywhere and anytime. Also, you can include links and URLs that give greater clarity and precise information about your selected Features.

Combining the digital portions might require a little bit of effort to create a single PDF with a cover sheet that you can share via email or from the cloud.

Alternately, you can print your Packet and place it in a nice-looking protective folder (plastic folder, clamp folder, three ring binder, etc.). You need one copy for each architect you interview, and one for each remodeler you interview.

Your Packet doesn't need to be professionally printed. But remember, you're the Boss, and you set the tone for the team you are assembling. If dog-eared, coffee-stained pages with handwritten lists is what they get from you, don't expect high-class, professionally printed proposals and communications from them.

Make your first impression a really good one.

The amount and quality of the information in a complete Project Packet will truly surprise and impress them. They'll know you are serious and that you understand what's about to happen. They will treat you with more respect as a result.

Your Project Packet is a clear, easy-to-understand summary of the project you desire and the price you are willing to pay to get those results. It brings everyone a clear understanding of the project that could not be obtained any other way.

So make your Project Packet look nice, and start the public portion of your remodeling journey on the best possible note.

Action Item #12:

Assemble and print out your Project Packet now.

Whether digital (as a single PDF file) or printed in a nice cover/binder, assemble multiple sets of your Project Packet now.

You will need a copy for *every* design professional and every remodeler you plan to interview. You'll get a better feel for those numbers as you read the next two sections, but five to ten copies would not be unreasonable.

Section 2:
CONSULT

When you contact professionals you might work with, you do so to **CONSULT** with them. You'll ask some specific questions and listen carefully to their answers. You'll try to discern who offers you the very best options while discarding average and poor options.

This section is devoted to the different types of professionals you are most likely to encounter while planning *a kitchen remodeling project*. I explain the pros and cons of each type of professional after discussing exactly what they offer you (and what they don't).

If you've ever asked yourself, "Who should I even call about my project?", I'm happy to say this section answers that question.

The section starts with the design pros you might encounter, and then covers the remodeling pros typically used for kitchen projects.

Chapter 11

Design Professionals

You have now prepared a thorough Project Packet which fully describes your proposed kitchen project. This includes your Elevator Pitch (describing the basic scope of work), Need List, Wish List, Budget, and Selection Table with major functions & features you're considering. You have also added some extra items as required by your circumstances (like a plot plan, HOA docs, and manufacturer spec sheets for appliances and other major choices you've made).

The next step is to select who you will talk to first.

If you are serious about getting design help with your kitchen, then you should know about the different types of designers who can help you with your kitchen. You really need to understand their strengths and weaknesses and the cost implications of each type of designer. I'll explain which design pros are right for your particular project and give you tips on interviewing them before committing to hire anyone.

Architects

Kitchen projects are occasionally part of a larger project (requiring an addition, or as part of a large project involving several rooms and areas). In this case architects are easily the most beneficial designers to work with.
Kitchen projects are occasionally part of a larger project (requiring an addition, or as part of a large project involving several rooms and areas). In this case architects are easily the most beneficial designers to work with.

Architects can work on interior-only projects, additions, and whole-home remodels. Technically they can be used for any size project, but they are typically used for larger, more complex projects because those project budgets more easily support the higher design expenses.

Who Are Architects?

An *architect* is a trained professional who plans, designs, and oversees the construction of buildings. The title of *architect* derives from the Greek words **arkhi** + **tekton**, meaning "chief master builder".

Since an architect's decisions affect public safety, architects working in the United States must be licensed. Before obtaining their license, architects endure years of technical university education, several years of internship for practical experience, and then a nine-part, four-day license examination.

Those are the minimum requirements to practice as an architect. They must be licensed in each state where they work. So if you hire an architect, always be sure they are licensed by your state.

What Do Architects Do?

In most remodeling situations, the architect is the ideal designer. This is due to their extensive training in all aspects of the home environment. They are trained to devise creative solutions for their clients that actually meet their needs. They also possess unique talents for three-dimensional problem solving, including how structural, plumbing, electrical, and mechanical systems combine within their design.

The biggest benefit of high-quality residential architects is their ability to mold the three-dimensional space of new and existing rooms together into one unified solution. When you are doing an addition, adding a floor to your home, or combining rooms together, architects alone have all the skills and legal qualifications you are likely to need.

There are also a couple drawbacks you should know about before you hire an architect to assist with your kitchen remodel. These include their potentially high cost, the amount of time their process takes, and their ability to design to your budget.

Cost – Architects cost more than any other design professionals you might meet. However, you also have the option to consult with them at an hourly rate, or to have them draw preliminary sketches of possible solutions for a low fixed cost. And you can hire them to do traditional full-service designs that include as-built drawings, a custom designed solution, and construction plans—all for a percentage of the total project cost.

Their fees are typically between 5 and 8 percent of the proposed project budget.

You can also hire your architect to provide supervision while the remodeler constructs the project, but you will pay additional fees for that service.

However, most modest kitchen remodeling projects don't have a budget large enough to cover the entire cost of the remodeling, let alone the additional cost of an architect.

Time – Architects do their interviews, field measurements, as-built drawings, and schematic designs before they produce the drawings and specifications needed to obtain bids or file for building permits. This entire process is typically done **before** homeowners hire a remodeler. The design and drawing process with an architect can be as few as thirty days and as long as a year for complex projects. This amount of time is not anticipated by most homeowners. Based on TV show remodeling, most homeowners assume that the design and remodeling process is very speedy, but this is not the case in real life.

Hitting the Budget – Architects are excellent at devising creative 3D solutions based on your needs, but they are terrible at estimating the cost of their designs. Please listen to this again carefully: most architects are BAD cost estimators of the projects they design. Few admit this, but I know this from personal experience. Don't blame architects as a group for this failing—they simply are not trained as estimators. Their skill set is quite large, but it usually does not include *accurate* remodeling estimating.

In a typical case, you can expect the *actual* price of their designs to be a minimum of 10 percent higher, and as much as 50 percent above your agreed upon budget.

And if you were wondering… it's impossible to trim 20 percent (or more) from a design and still get a result that resembles the initial design. Removing that much value from any remodeling project mandates that it be redesigned, and still the project scope may need to be reduced.

In fact, to reduce an over-budget design by as little as 10 percent requires significant compromises on the stated design goals, and often leaves homeowners quite disappointed. There is just no way to feel enthusiastic about a gutted, shrunken project that was reduced in scope because the initial design was too costly based on faulty estimating by the architect.

And I have **never** seen a contract that required the architect to redesign the project if the initial attempt failed to hit the agreed budget. As unfair as it is, do-overs require you to pay additional fees for additional designs.

To recap—architects are the best design professionals to work with on your larger and more complex kitchen remodels, especially ones that involve multiple rooms or an addition. But you should understand their cost, the time they require, and the potential for budget overruns before you interview or hire one.

Don't be discouraged by these drawbacks if you really like the upside benefits of using an architect to design your new kitchen. In the chapters about different remodeler types, I'll share a special option that will likely allow you to work with an architect after all! And that option eliminates most of the drawbacks mentioned above while you still get to enjoy the creative and customized solutions that architects offer.

Other Architectural Designers

There are people who call themselves architectural designers and/or drafts people. These folks are untrained, unlicensed individuals without the formal training and skills you need for a proper kitchen design.

Seek out other types of help if you want the best results, and avoid these so-called designers.

Interior Design Professionals

Interior design pros fall into two camps: interior designers and interior decorators.

In general terms, interior designers create highly functional spaces based on the customer's preferences and behaviors. Decorators, on the other hand, fashionably manipulate the furnishings and finishes of an interior space.

Interior design-related projects usually involve the content of rooms (cabinetry & tops, built-ins, furniture, etc.), but they seldom involve the technical trades and aspects of construction such as plumbing, HVAC, electric service, or structural manipulation. As a result, the jobs that interior design professionals do are typically interior only, and non-structural projects.

Interior Designers

Twenty-eight of the fifty states (plus DC and Puerto Rico) now recognize interior designers by either licensing, registration, or title restrictions. The term *interior designer* is not protected (it was deemed too generic), so most states that allow registration or title protection only protect the term ***registered interior designer*** or ***certified interior designer***.

Professionally recognized interior designers must have obtained a university design education, done mandatory professional practice time, and passed the national NCIDQ exam (National Council for Interior Design Qualification), and then they must remain current through continuing education.
Since states are constantly amending requirements for interior design professionals, you can find the current status of each state here:
http://advocacy.iida.org/#interiordesignlaws.

Interior designers are formally trained to design creative interior spaces that are also safe, functional, and compliant with building local codes. Their skill set and services go far beyond making color selections and furniture layouts, which surprises many homeowners.

Their contribution *can* be as simple as the clever re-arrangement of how space is used, to projects that require technical expertise like window and door placement, acoustics, and lighting. But their skill set does not typically include exterior work, structural modifications, or coordination with the major trades (HVAC, plumbing, electric). For this reason, when working on major projects, interior designers often partner with architects.

For design advice on things like furniture layouts based on room size, finishes, lighting, color, and interior room detailing, interior designers could be your best choice of professional designers. This is most likely when your renovation includes your kitchen and other interior rooms.

Otherwise, it is unlikely that you would hire an interior designer to design most typical kitchen remodels.

Interior Decorators

Decorators, unlike professionally recognized interior designers, are not licensed or registered professionals. There is no educational or training requirement for people to call themselves an interior decorator.

The range of services offered by decorators includes designing interior layouts or advising on the surface treatments in rooms (textures, paint colors, wallpapers, blinds and curtains, flooring materials, tile, etc.) and the furniture and accessories used to achieve a particular style or look.

Decorators typically have contacts in both the supply and installation trades, and they can help get their designs priced or installed. Sometimes they are aligned with specific brands, for which they can get significant discounts, but they may also have exclusive agreements to use only those brands or products. Be sure to inquire about this if you consider using a decorator.

As I mentioned with Interior Designers, it's not terribly likely you'll need or use a decorator for typical kitchen remodels.

Pro Tip:

As with most design professionals, you can hire an interior designer (or decorator) to consult with you and offer advice on colors, textures, and materials if you are confused while you try to coordinate flooring, cabinets, countertops, backsplashes, and paint colors in your kitchen!

Specialty Designers

There are a number of specialty designers that only work in one specific field. The most common specialists are kitchen & bath designers, which include both certified and uncertified practitioners. The two other designers you might consider are lighting designers and tile designers.

Kitchen & Bath Designers

Kitchen and bath designers specialize in kitchen and bathroom design. They can help you with almost anything kitchen or bathroom related. They can design the new layouts, do detailed cabinet design, and help you with appliance selection, plumbing fixture selection, tile design, etc. In other words, if it has something to do with kitchens or bathrooms, these designers can really help.

Your big problem is that kitchen and bath designers are not all licensed, so the title *kitchen and bath designer* is not restricted. This also means that **anyone** can design kitchens and bathrooms, including those who are untrained and uneducated. In fact, the vast majority of people designing kitchens and baths **are not** formally trained, making it tougher for you to identify the best designers.

Most so-called kitchen designers you will encounter are not—they are just semi-skilled sales people who are primarily concerned with selling you cabinets. They use computer software to arrange new layouts, they show you pretty 3D images, and then price and order cabinets.

Once again, in the case of this type of kitchen and bath designer, the term *designer* is a misnomer. They appear in every big box home center and retail cabinet showroom you visit. So don't forget that they are salespeople with nifty cabinet design software, trying to sell as much product as possible.

While some great kitchen designers do reside on staff inside retail cabinet showrooms, many are unaffiliated with any particular showroom or retail brand. They can typically offer significantly more assistance to the consumer, with a fuller set of design services.

Despite the fact kitchen and bath designers are not licensed, there does exist a group of truly professional designers with formal training and official certification.

Certified designers have been instructed by national organizations that issue training courses and seminars which certify that their trainees meet high quality standards. What the designers earn through these courses is not a license or a state registration, but it is a guarantee that the certified individual has undergone a rigorous regimen of formal training before passing the exam and becoming certified.

The National Kitchen and Bath Association (NKBA), founded in 1963, is one national organization that certifies kitchen and bath designers. They have over sixty thousand certified members (CKBDs, Certified Kitchen and Bath Designers; or CMKBDs, Certified Master Kitchen and Bath Designers). NKBA also accredits many college and university design programs, so students who graduate have a leg up on the certification process.

Their CKBD certification requires a minimum of sixty hours of approved classroom education and three to five years of full-time experience, followed by passing an academic design exam.

Many large, privately-owned kitchen and bath shops have a certified designer or two on staff. Some of the corporate shops will too, though you'll have to seek them out specifically. Other designer employees in those same stores may be seeking certification, or just working as cabinet salespeople.

To find out if a particular showroom or business has certified designers, just call and ask (or ask when visiting) if any of their designers are NKBA certified.

Whichever kitchen designer you choose, the most important factor is their experience. Those who have designed hundreds of kitchens, who pride themselves on knowing the details of the major cabinet lines, and who stay abreast of appliance trends will be the most help to you. Never hesitate to ask to see samples of kitchens they have personally designed. Each kitchen design was crafted to meet someone else's needs, but you should notice a trend of great layouts and fun features that excites you. If not, move on.

Your goal is to avoid cabinet salespeople with only some training on their fancy software, and instead find a true kitchen designer with a solid grasp of the factors affecting high-quality custom kitchen design.

You need someone who exhibits knowledge and experience to go along with some creativity so they can deliver solutions that delight you while addressing all your basic needs. Do not settle for a salesperson; seek out a certified designer, or at least a designer on their way to certification.

With regard to the shops themselves, any one cabinet showroom has a limited brand selection (lines of cabinets, plumbing fixtures, appliances, and flooring). Don't be surprised if a shop has just three to five total brands, each with one or two lines of cabinets. Generally, they will have one builder-grade or entry-level cabinet brand, two or so semi-custom brands, and a couple fully-custom brands. This allows them to handle the vast majority of situations that homeowners require.

A one-stop shop for all the basic kitchen materials is a fabulous idea, but it would be impractically large and terribly expensive to bring so many products and experts together in one building or location.

A certified kitchen designer has the expertise to advise you on flooring, tile, appliances, and plumbing fixtures in addition to designing your new layout. They should be able to help you make choices where those other products dovetail together into your new kitchen design.

As with architects and other professionals, you need to shop around! All people and their companies come with different philosophies, talents, personalities, etc.

You alone determine who is easiest to communicate with, who sees your vision clearly, and who has the expertise necessary to help you with your kitchen.

> **Pro Tip:** Be aware that your countertops, appliances, flooring, and even plumbing fixtures may come from other specialty showrooms. You might order your plumbing fixtures from a plumbing supply shop since cabinet showrooms can't really showcase the same volume of products as a plumbing showroom. This is also the case with flooring, tile, and lighting options.
>
> The bottom line is that a cabinet showroom makes and sells cabinets—not flooring, countertops, or faucets. When you buy those products from the cabinet vendor you may save yourself a few steps, but you will spend more than when buying your tops from a countertop shop, and your tile from a tile shop, etc.
>
> Everything for your kitchen will probably not come from one location. If saving time is your goal, then one-stop shopping at the cabinet showroom works. If saving money is your goal, the best prices usually come from the individual product shops.

Tile Designers

There are no licenses or certifications for these folks. However, if you find a tile salesperson with years of experience, a grasp of their product lines, and a talent for design, then they can help you mix and match materials, colors, sizes, and shapes into a nifty layout for your floor or backsplash.

When looking for a tile designer, ask to meet with the most experienced designer when you visit a tile showroom, and see how that person's advice feels. There's no other way to know how good they are except to talk to them and perhaps see samples of their work (or call references).

Similar to cabinet designers, tile designers work in shops that have six or eight tile manufacturers and lots of shapes and sizes in each line. Nobody has "all the tile" in their catalog or showroom. So if there's something very specific that you've seen and want to consider (a particular tile size, shape, style), bring a picture of it, so they can show you their shop's most comparable tile.

Lighting Designers

High-quality lighting design enhances any architectural experience. You don't want to just settle for a fixture in the middle of each room's ceiling like it is 1950 all over again. So don't let remodelers design your lighting, and don't do it yourself.

Then who should you use? If you don't work with an architect, seek out experienced lighting designers with lots of residential design experience as you visit your nearby lighting showrooms. These folks are not licensed, registered, or certified, but you can walk into any shop and ask to meet their top residential designer. That should do the trick. This way you won't get a salesperson; you'll get a designer who can take the plans that others have drawn for you and enhance them with light.

Undoubtedly, you won't need or even like all the types of high-tech lighting available today. But the improved methods for lighting kitchens today compared to just ten or fifteen years ago are amazing. Dimmable LEDs in the 2,700–3,000K range are everywhere and can be used as task lighting from the ceiling, from under the cabinets, or from fixtures. LED bulbs (lamps) last much longer, are cool to the touch (very little heat is produced), and cost just pennies to use—even if lit all day long.

So, explore the world of options open to you in a lighting showroom or design studio, and have fun!

Design It Yourself

My advice on do-it-yourself design is this: **don't**.

Trust design professionals to devise a creative solution for your kitchen that addresses your needs. They do it for a living. They are better at solving three-dimensional problems that satisfy client needs than you will ever be. And they are familiar with code compliance and specialty trade nuances, unlike you.

That being said, I love working with a savvy, well-informed homeowner. One way I have seen folks become significantly more in tune with their projects (no, it's NOT by watching HGTV!) is to measure and draw a solution yourself. They get a feel for the true room size, wall thicknesses, door and window locations, cabinets, and furniture by doing this.

However, if you are going to draw your own solution, I'd suggest picking up a great piece of 3D residential design software for your computer. The software I've used for the past twenty-five years is called Chief Architect (a very expensive tool for remodeling professionals). But they also make a fabulous, homeowner-friendly, easy-to-learn drawing software called Home Designer Software by Chief Architect. There are different consumer versions and even an option to rent their professional software at a monthly rate it if you are serious.

There are many other brands and types of CAD software, but none that I have ever seen that are as easy to learn and use and which give fast results in 2D and 3D. The complexity of most CAD products means you'll never really get it to work properly—and it will be a waste of your time and money.

If you do try measuring your existing home (or kitchen) and then designing a potential solution for your project, I have one critical piece of advice: **Don't drink the Kool-Aid!**

By that I mean, don't fall in love with **your solution**. Remember, this is just an exercise. You're doing it for fun. Do it for the experience and knowledge to be gained.

Then work with your design professionals, who will design your new kitchen significantly better, taking into consideration many more variables, to craft a customized solution for you and your family.

Chapter 12

Designer Costs

There are some rules of thumb you can apply to the relative cost of design professionals. They go like this:

Architects cost more for the same task than an interior designer, and both cost more than a certified specialty designer. While they are all registered or licensed or certified, architects can do more and have a broader professional skill set and therefore cost more than the others.

Within each category (architectural, interior, and specialty), those who are licensed, certified, or registered are all costlier than those without formal education and training in those fields. The only reason you would deliberately choose to work with an unlicensed or uncertified professional is that you know them personally and you're convinced that their design aesthetic is perfect for your situation. Or when you just need an opinion and not a complete design.

However, if you need design plans for the project, and if those plans will be used to obtain a building permit, then the architect is the only design specialist you should use. If you hire anyone else, you'll probably still pay an architect or engineer to "seal" the permit drawings.

Design professionals can charge you in three ways:
- based on an hourly rate,
- by the specific task, or
- by the complete project.

Which one you choose (and **you should choose**, not them) is based on the extent of work you need performed. If you need opinions and quick ideas, hire by the hour. A quick hand sketch or two of a potential layout with some notes on materials lends itself to hiring with a task-based-price (a smaller fixed fee).

Then, if you need a full design, with bid or permit documents and assistance with bidding or obtaining materials or contractors for the work, that's the full monty. You will get advice, a preliminary design, some modifications, a final edited design, and all necessary project drawings and documentation—all for a set fee.

Each professional prices their work differently, so **ask** them about their fees for various scopes of work when you first interview them.

It is important that you always know what you're getting in exchange for your payment!

With the exception of hiring someone for an hour or two of advice (or Q&A), you should always get your agreements with building professionals in writing (a signed contract with the pro you choose). The agreement should say what they are providing (design services, permit plans, documents, bid specifications, prices, etc.). And if there should be revisions included after the initial design, that must be mentioned in the agreement. The pros don't want to perform endless edits, so the language should state the limits on revisions in simple terms. If you don't understand their terms and jargon, ask for the terms to be in plain English. You must understand what you will receive in exchange for the fee you pay!

Chapter 13

Hiring a Designer

It helps to know what to expect before you make the call and set up a meeting. This chapter gives several tips and suggestions on the best steps to take after you decide to work with design professionals on your kitchen.

First and foremost, you always want to hire those who have done this for many years. While everyone needs a first client or a first large project, never let your kitchen be their first big project. Besides, businesses that last seven years are past the most difficult financial hurdles and are typically well-established in the community and the industry.

With that in mind, here are some ideas to consider before contacting designers about your kitchen:

- Hire the person with the best credentials **in the specific area of expertise that you need**. If you're after help with interior color, you don't need an architect, you need someone who does room colors every day.
- When you need help with tile patterns or cabinet layouts, don't waste time with a higher-paid generalist, go to the expert. Get the big design from the big pro; then get the specific design from a specialist.
- Architects, interior design pros, and most specialty designers can be hired by the hour or by the project/job/design. When you need more than a short consultation, get a full-job price quote. Make sure it covers the design, the drawings, and your rights to use them any way you wish. Don't hire designers by the hour. It gets *very* expensive, because you have no control over their time. It's smart to have a maximum price built-in.

Before you hire ANY designer, see designs they have done for projects similar to yours. While you might not like the style or the colors—since those were the choices of other homeowners—be sure you like the cleverness and the style of the designer you choose. Also, call their former clients (more than one) to be certain that working with the designer was an easy and pleasant experience.

Pro Tip:

Nearly all design professionals offer a free initial meeting to discuss a potential project. Some will do so at your home, others at their office. Take full advantage of that time to thoroughly interview them and assess their skill and personality. Never be pressured to hire anyone immediately. Always sleep on it.

Finally, call their references to be sure they had easy communication and a great working relationship with the pro you are considering.

Keep in mind that design professionals come in all shapes, sizes, genders, and personalities. Be certain you select one with whom you can speak plainly, one who sees your project vision and is not trying to steer you in their direction. Be sure you have good rapport with them, because two-way conversation and idea sharing are essential. And remember, there are dozens of others who will be thrilled to work with you, so turn down anyone that is not ideal for you.

Finally, never work on a handshake. Make sure you are very clear about what you get in exchange for their fee. Get it in writing, and sign a contract with them. If revisions to the initial design are included, the contract should clearly say so.

Again, I can't stress this enough: know what you will get **before** you sign.

PRO TIP:

If you only need advice (not a full project design or a complete set of permit drawings), then just pay for advice! You can usually hire the professionals discussed here for an hour or two of consultation.

Have an architect come to your house and advise you which walls are bearing walls and need structural solutions for their removal (and which don't). Or ask them for a simple hand sketch for a possible layout for the new kitchen, eating, and mudroom entry, etc.

When your remodeling is nearing completion, bring a decorator out to talk about finished flooring colors, paint colors, wallpaper, and window treatments. Do it as a consult, not a full design. One or two hours while you take notes about their suggestions (like sources and brand names) should answer your questions without committing you to a large fee and more drawings than you really need.

Just pay them to consult if consultation is all you really need!

Chapter 14

Remodeling Professionals

The single biggest mistake a homeowner can make is to hire the wrong remodeler.

That bears repeating.

The single biggest mistake a homeowner can make is to hire the wrong remodeler.

Choosing the wrong remodeler leads to more problems, delays, cost overruns, and project failures than all the other mistakes combined.

It seems so obvious, right?

So the question now becomes "How do I *avoid* hiring the wrong remodeler?"

The best place to start is with a clear understanding of the right type of remodeler for your job, your budget, and your temperament.

Types of Remodelers

What the typical homeowner doesn't know is that there are different **types** of remodeling contractors. Some companies do large volumes of work, while others do small volumes. Some take on only specific kinds of projects. Still others have business models that make them more or less attractive for certain project types.

Typically, homeowners call eight or ten remodelers in order to get three or four to show up. Why is that? Simple. Most of those called have a different specialty than the owner's project. Owners routinely mismatch their project type with the remodeler's specialty.

It's not really the homeowner's fault, however. Sure, they called the wrong remodelers. But why? Because most remodelers mislead folks into thinking they do more project types than they really do. A specialist actually does far more of the thing they specialize in than anything else. But what do the advertisements and websites of most home improvement contractors say they "specialize" in? **EVERYTHING!**

You and I both know that's not possible.

I am willing to bet that you didn't know there are many different types of remodelers. So how should you fight your way past misleading advertising to find those that are truly perfect for your kitchen project?

Kitchen Experts Only

This section introduces to you *only* remodelers that typically perform kitchen renovations. Just like all doctors once had the same basic medical school training, most remodelers have done a few kitchens. However, your goal is to hire someone who does kitchens all the time.

The advantage you gain by hiring a kitchen specialist is huge. Their familiarity with kitchens works to your advantage. They know the common problems that crop up and how to overcome them. They know the right way to perform the tasks required without screw-ups. They are more time and material efficient than those who only perform the occasional kitchen renovation. And the skills of their staff will be specifically geared toward kitchens.

The following review of remodelers provides you with the key information needed to identify the best remodeler type(s) for your specific project. You will include and exclude some of the remodeler types using your Project Packet information.

Some kitchens will be part of a larger project or an addition, and some will remain within the four walls of the current kitchen. Those two projects ideally call for different types of remodelers. The next few chapters help you determine which remodeler type is ideal for your kitchen project.

Professionals Only

Only ever work with professional home improvement contractors. Simply getting paid to remodel does **not** make a company professional. And it certainly does not mean they perform up to professional standards. The very best remodelers make a good living, produce excellent work, and have loads of happy customers. They do it over and over for years, establishing an excellent track record in this difficult business.

Furthermore, true professionals have a very caring approach to their work, to their customer relationships, and to the law. The remodelers you consider must all be licensed or registered as required by law, and should all be fully insured. I'll review these two factors in the next chapter. It seems so obvious to say never work with any unlicensed remodeler or anyone who is not properly insured, yet it happens hundreds of times each day.

You should only ever hire contractors who obtain all necessary permits and inspections. Never consider using a contractor that suggests going without a building permit or inspections when they are required.

Of course, obtaining a building permit and getting inspections adds a little time and expense to your project. But they ensure that your remodeler works within approved code standards. Think of inspections and code compliance as the local jurisdiction looking out for your well-being, helping to protect your investment and your home.

Explore Unique Circumstances Early

If you have unique circumstances or needs that may rule out some companies, it's best to find out as soon as possible. Since unique circumstances are, well, unique, I can't possibly explain them all, but I will give a few examples.

One example would be if you wish to use the direct-pay option (where you pay subcontractors directly with your checkbook or credit card) for your project. In this case, you should investigate that option with the company's salesman before setting an appointment, and then review it again during the interview so everyone is clear. Another example would be that your schedule has unique deadlines that affect the start or end of a project (a wedding being hosted in the backyard next summer, old friends visiting for two weeks from Germany, you're all away on vacation for a month, you need to live in the house and stage the project in two distinct phases). These types of situations would need to be discussed in advance, and again in the interview.

Another unique condition would be if you have a friend or family member who owns a company that you want to participate in the project as a subcontractor (because they are giving you a "deal"). In this case, you must be sure that the remodelers that you select to interview will work with your relative. Some may not. Many spend years cultivating relationships with their subs and don't want to work with anyone else. They also have no control over your buddy or brother-in-law as far as scheduling and quality go.

If you need your remodeler to pause mid-project to allow YOU to perform a phase of the project, you MUST get that approved in advance. Messing with the schedule, especially in a non-skilled, open-ended time frame, could well eliminate a lot of your best choices—so pick and choose your unique circumstances carefully.

These are just a few examples that can guide you. But if you have these or any other unusual needs or requests, you will want to call or drop by the remodeling company's office to ask in advance. It's best to find out early if your special needs are a problem that precludes you from working together, before wasting everyone's time.

Chapter 15

Licenses and Insurance

Remodeling Licensing

Some of you live in states or jurisdictions where remodeling contractors are NOT required to have a remodeling license. This makes it more difficult for you to verify the quality of your prospective hires. You'll need to do some extra work to verify that each remodeler considered is financially stable and serious about their reputation and has a long tenure in the community with a lot of happy clients.

Below is a quick rundown of the licensing requirements in the US, at the time of publishing:

- Twenty-nine states in the US require remodelers to obtain a state-issued license before they can perform any home-improvement work. Working on homes without a license in most of these states is a violation of the law punishable by fines and/or jail time. The licensing requirements vary by state, and you should look up your state licensing board to learn more about your state licensing requirements.

- Idaho, Iowa, New Jersey, and Washington don't license home improvement contractors, but they register them instead. This covers all home improvement contractors and occurs at the state level. Registration is not as strict as licensing, but it means that the state maintains control over the industry and the practitioners. As I cautioned above, if you live in one of these states, only work with registered remodelers, and check them out with your state agency before inviting them to your home for an interview!

- In eight states, they license or register remodelers at the local level only, not at the state level. The jurisdiction may be a city, county, or town, but in order to operate legally, home improvement contractors must be registered or licensed to work in these jurisdictions. These states include: Colorado, Delaware, Illinois, Indiana, Kansas, Missouri, Ohio, and Vermont.

- EXTREMELY LIMITED local registration or licensing in selected cities and areas occurs in four states: Kentucky, New Hampshire, South Dakota, and Wyoming. Outside of the handful of municipalities requiring registration here, there is no current regulation of the industry in these states.

- Five states: Maine, New York, Oklahoma, Texas, and Wisconsin, have NO licensing or registration at the state or local level.

Unless you live in one of the five states with no licensing or registration, you should *always* call or go online to determine if your state, county, or town requires remodeler licensing or registration. If so, always verify that your contractor's licensed name and number matches on every document they show you and that their license is currently active. **This is the first and best method of protecting your money and your home any time you remodel.**

Choosing to ignore this advice can be a recipe for disaster. Many states that license remodelers disallow court cases against unlicensed contractors, eliminating any legal recourse you might have had. It is a huge gamble to hire unlicensed remodelers and should be avoided. There is no possible outcome that is worth putting your investment, your home, and your family at risk.

Pro Tip:

This site has information on remodeler licensing in every US state (and DC) and gives links to contact each state's remodeling board:

https://www.homeadvisor.com/r/state-by-state-licensing-requirements/

Are They Insured?

Every remodeler you consider working with should be fully insured. There are two critical types of insurance that most remodelers must carry: liability insurance and worker's compensation insurance.

The liability insurance covers your home and property if an accident occurs during the performance of the project. The worker's compensation insurance covers jobsite accidents for their employees.

I go into more detail about insurance and how you can verify that each remodeler you interview is properly insured in the CHOOSE section of this book.

Critical Remodeling Mistake #2

Identify and hire only the right TYPE of remodeler for your project.

Remodeling companies come in many different sizes and with many different specialties. *You can't get the right results if you choose the wrong remodeler.*

Pay very close to the remodeler types so you can identify the right remodeler type(s) for your project. Only once you know the right type of contractor for your job can you move forward selecting companies to interview.

Chapter 16

Remodeler Types

I mentioned that most homeowners don't know there are different **types** of remodeling contractors. But intuitively this should already be in our minds.

Think about selecting a doctor. You don't just open the phone book to "doctors" and select anyone with an MD degree when you need help. You first consider what your need is, and then you specifically look for a doctor who works in that specialty.

When you need help with a sore throat, you don't make an appointment with an optometrist. When you hurt an ankle, you don't visit an ENT. When you have digestive issues, you don't consult with a podiatrist.

Each of these physicians is a medical doctor. Each of them studied and work on the same human body. And I suppose each of them could offer some generic advice. But since they became specialized, they spend every day working with the specific needs of patients in a very narrow field. This specialization allows them to provide expert help to folks with a specific problem.

This same thing happens in remodeling. Most remodelers actually prefer to work on one type, or one size of project. Some specialize in basements, some in kitchens & baths, some in additions, some in whole-home renovations. Some only do roofing, or siding, or windows. Some perform odd jobs.

So let's look at the different types of remodelers that could be considered for your kitchen project.

Design-Build Remodelers

What Exactly Is Design-Build?

The term *design-build* refers to the joining together of an architectural design team with the building construction team. The idea was first used in commercial construction so developers could reduce the time it took to get a project designed and constructed while keeping it on budget during the process. The biggest benefit of design-build is the cooperation between these two camps.

In the traditional construction process, architects do all their design and drawings first, get paid, and then put their construction drawings out for bids. The architects are not on the same team with the contractors, either figuratively or literally.

Traditional projects take longer to get constructed due to the linear process of having the entire project fully designed, and only then being able to obtain construction estimates and proposals. Revisions would then go back to the architect and need to be rebid by the contractors—all before a construction agreement could be signed.

Design-build allows the design to be estimated early and accurately and then re-estimated at all stages of re-design. This keeps the project budget in check throughout the process since the design and estimating of projects is cooperative.

Another significant savings that design-build (DB) offers over the traditional architect plus remodeler method is this: When the design, planning, and estimating take place in a collaborative team setting, the initial designs are always better, and the estimated cost is much more likely to be near the budget.

With the traditional, linear process, the total cost to the owner is always higher. The owner pays the full price of two separate sets of professionals, and very often pays them additional fees to perform revisions when the initial design is rejected or is too far over budget. In addition, the traditional process is much slower (takes longer) than the design-build process since both sets of professionals do their thing independently one after the other and not cooperatively.

Design-build offers owners significant time and cost savings (due to a streamlined and cooperative process) and also delivers better designs that are much closer to the budget.

Large remodeling contractors started offering "design-build" services to homeowners in the 1990s. Since then, "design-build" has become the hottest marketing phrase in the industry. There's almost no remodeler that doesn't tout their "design-build services" in their ads and on their website. This, of course, further confuses homeowners who didn't know what design-build was to begin with!

By now you are probably wondering if it is even possible that all those remodelers are truly design-build companies, combining architectural design with traditional construction? No. It's not possible.

Extremely few of today's remodeling companies that claim to be design-build use architects to do their designs and permit drawings. And almost no so-called design-build firms have architects on staff. This begs the question: "If they are not using architects, then who is doing the designing?" This brilliant question has a simple and alarming answer: You don't know! But you can bet in most instances that the designers are not architects, and the remodeler is not actually a design-build remodeler.

Homeowners get hoodwinked by these phony design-build companies because they are unaware that the designer is not an architect, but there's an allure of lower fees (since there are no separate architect fees involved). The homeowner has no idea that $1,000 or $2,000 in design fees from an architect is an extremely smart investment and typically delivers far superior solutions than those from a generic remodeling designer.

There is one legitimate design-build situation besides the architect being employed by the remodeling company. Many traditional remodelers (a type of remodeler that I discuss in the next chapter) can operate on select large projects as a true design-build company by partnering with an outside architect. By doing this, they create an architect-remodeler team to serve their large-project clients. This way they are offering true architectural services to their customers, without the high-priced architect being a full-time employee. In this case, remodelers charge design fees to cover the architect's costs.

Even though this homeowner pays design fees plus the full remodeling price, the benefits of the true design-build process are all in effect. The architect and remodeler are on the same team, both working for the homeowner. Together they offer increased speed from design through construction, as well as cooperative design and estimating that results in more on-budget projects. And don't forget that the solutions are usually more creative with a licensed residential architect.

This design-build partnership concept is typically used for large projects because the budget for most small projects cannot support an architect's design fees. The remodeler must generate enough money to pay the architect, and they typically do this by charging design fees to the client.

As previously stated, true design-build remodeling delivers a superior solution when compared to non-architect designs, so it should be seriously considered for any large or complex kitchen project. Additions that include kitchens, whole-home remodels with kitchens, many upscale kitchens, and those being expanded into adjacent rooms would all qualify for design-build consideration.

Beware!

Like I mentioned earlier, the majority of today's so-called design-build remodelers **are not**! Instead, they are traditional remodelers who produce medium or large projects, and they only use the phrase "design-build" to attract clients. No architect is involved in their design process.

So who does the designing if not a licensed architect? The sad answer is that a random employee on the remodeler's staff does it. If you get lucky, they might have some CAD or drafting experience. If you are really lucky, they spent a few years studying architecture before quitting school to start work in remodeling.

But whatever a remodeling company calls itself, when no architect is involved, you are not getting true design-build services or benefits.

If your project justifies a design-build company, do not even consider using a phony "design-build" company. Your kitchen's design will be only as good as the talent of their "designer", something that is impossible for a layman to discern.

If your project could benefit from an architect's design, then hire an architect and bid the project out, or hire a **real** design-build remodeling company that uses licensed architects.

It's always worth the price you pay to get top-quality professional design paired with a top-quality construction experience.

Cost Implications

The remodeling costs of most design-build remodeling companies is very similar to or just slightly higher than those of a traditional large-project remodeling company (the next type of remodeling professional we will review). And it is usually well below the total cost of hiring a separate architect plus a remodeler.

True design-build companies have higher overhead than other remodelers when they have architects on staff. But when a remodeler partners with outside architects, their overhead and your remodeling costs should be comparable with other similarly-sized standard remodelers.

When a remodeler uses outside architects to provide design-build services, you should expect to pay a design fee plus the remodeling construction costs.

The design fee charged by most design-build remodelers is based on the architect's cost. Typically, these fees are much lower those you pay when hiring the same architect directly. For simple design sketches or schematic ideas, the price could range from $500 to $1,500. For design and permit drawings, it might reach $2,500 to $4,000 (and more for larger, more complex projects). This is considerably lower than what most licensed architects charge their clients. Additionally, the "team" gets owner feedback and can provide estimates of the evolving design, keeping the project much closer to the budget than the ordinary architect plus remodeler process.

Occasionally, design-build remodelers may offer a unique pricing structure where a portion of the design fee is credited against the cost of the remodeling contract. This is a win-win for the customer and the remodeler. So if your project is large or complex and you want an architect to design your solution, check with some highly-rated design-build remodelers first. Always inquire up front about the design fees (what those fees cover and who owns the rights to their designs) and whether any of the design fee is credited toward the remodeling contract.

Drawbacks

While design-build remodelers offer many advantages to their customers, there are a couple unique drawbacks to using a DB company. These drawbacks include the following:

- **You Choose Just One** – You can't get ideas, designs, and prices from several DB companies and then deliberate who to use for the remodeling. This is due to the fact that there are usually significant **design fees** just to get these folks to partner with you on your project (before anyone even lifts a pencil). Then, once you put one or two thousand dollars into the new design, it's not generally wise to break that relationship and shop elsewhere. Neither is it advisable to hire two or three DBs to provide you with several preliminary designs and estimates before choosing one to use. The obvious reason for this is the large up-front cost of multiple design fees and the contracts necessary to get them all involved.

- **There's No Bidding** – Most uninformed homeowners think, hear, or read that they should get several bids in order to know their project is priced well. I'll deal with the accuracy of that statement later in the book. But the bottom line is this: you can't compare prices between providers if they are true design-build companies. So you will need to do your company investigations up front before you sign the initial design contract and partner with one DB remodeler. Part of your investigation of each DB company being considered is how often their clients' projects wind up near or below the initial budget.

- **Ownership of the Design** – Typically, even if you pay design fees, the architect and/or the remodeler will retain the rights to the design. If this is the case, you cannot walk away from the partnership and hire a different remodeler to construct the project you had designed by them. This is a big deal since you spent a large design fee and have no right to use the drawings (without paying an additional amount for that privilege). This situation is typical, but not universal. My advice is to ask every DB remodeler you consider using (or their architect) about the rights to the design and drawings. WARNING! Obviously, asking this question raises a red flag to the remodeler, since they fear that you are only interested in an inexpensive design and you might walk away and build the project with another remodeler. But you need to know this information before you sign up or pay anything.

PRO TIP

What will you get for your money? It's critical to know which design-build services and products you get in exchange for your design fees. What's even more critical is finding out *before* you sign and pay anyone. One thing you must receive for your fees are the rights to use the design and drawings as you like (with them or with someone else). This needs to be spelled out in an agreement that you can review ahead of time.

Also find out how many design ideas or design revisions the agreement includes. You can't get endless revisions, but you might not like everything about the first solution. You may need to have a couple veto votes during the design phase, before the additional fees kick in.

Finally, with regard to the products you receive, do you get printed sets of drawings and a written spec with allowances? If their design is digital only (like Google Sketch-Up or other software), then it does you no good—unless that same remodeler builds the project. So ask for printed drawings and notes/specs.

One of Your Best Bets

Design-build remodelers are essentially medium and large-project traditional remodeling companies that use licensed architects for their designs. Those architects could be employees but are more likely to be independent professionals that partner with the remodeler for this exact scenario.

If your kitchen will be large or complex, or will be part of an addition, or will be combined with an adjacent room, then true design-build companies are an excellent choice for you. For example, if your project budget is $60,000 (or larger) or your project includes some structural modifications to your home, then you will be very well served by using a true design-build remodeler.

When you just want an architect-designed kitchen project and you're willing to pay **a little more** to get professional design combined with top-notch remodeling—then design-build is a great option.

But when the budget is tight and every dollar needs to go toward construction, this option may be too costly. If this is your case, don't lose all hope. There's one more professional design and construction combination yet to come that is right for many typical kitchen projects!

Traditional Remodelers

Traditional remodelers make up the majority of all remodeling professionals. They work on a wide range of projects, from one or two-day duration jobs up to luxury projects costing hundreds of thousands.

For the sake of this discussion, I'd like to break them down into smaller groups. Remodelers can be analyzed or grouped in several ways: by revenue, by size (the number of employees), and by the dollar size of their typical project. How much they make each year and how many employees they have matter very little when you are trying to find remodelers to work with. So I prefer to look at their typical project size to distinguish which ones might be right for your project.

I sort traditional remodeling companies into large, medium, and small project sizes. So their typical (or average) project will be either high priced (large), medium priced (medium), or low priced (small).

Large Project Remodelers

For us, the distinction *large project* covers jobs with a price range from about $65,000 and up. These tend to be the same size projects that architects may design and that design-build remodelers like to perform. In fact, when homeowners hire architects to draw complete projects, large traditional remodelers and design-build remodelers are often called on to bid on those projects for the architects. The singular difference between a large-project remodeling company and a true design-build remodeler is the lack of an architect on staff.

As a result, the designers at traditional remodeling companies are typically employees who wear other hats (like owner, salesperson, or production manager). This makes it impossible for you to assess and compare their design ability, experience, or training. For this reason, large traditional remodelers are never your first choice when high-quality design is a critical factor for your project.

In most cases, large traditional remodelers' everyday projects involve large and complex additions or projects with multiple interior rooms involved. Projects that exceed $65,000 are large projects by almost anyone's definition. And many large, complex, and upscale kitchens can exceed that figure easily.

To review, the large-project traditional remodeler routinely works on higher cost projects than the other traditional remodeling contractors. And when you're needing a more complex project constructed, you want a company that does it routinely and with great success.

Medium Project Remodelers

Just as we used project size to define large-project remodelers, we'll do the same for medium- and small-project remodelers as well.

Let's start with medium-project remodelers. These companies typically perform projects from $30,000 to about $75,000. As a result, their project scope differs from large-project remodelers.

Medium-project remodelers don't typically perform two-story additions or whole-house remodeling projects and seldom if ever add new floors to existing homes. They might do so occasionally, but their bread-and-butter project is a smaller, less complex project. And we're looking for remodelers that do your project type and size all the time.

For the most part, these remodelers do conventional additions with some other interior and exterior revisions thrown in. They might perform a basement finishing project (perhaps with a bedroom, bathroom, or kitchenette). You might use them for a bedroom suite over an existing garage. And they often perform modest kitchen additions, kitchen remodels, and significant-sized interior remodeling projects. They will also take on multiple smaller projects in combination, done under one contract.

Small Project Remodelers

Small-project remodelers typically work on jobs from about $5,000 to $40,000. They might work on projects such as powder rooms, hallway bath remodels, small-budget kitchens, screened porches, basements, and small one-room additions. These listed projects are not exclusive to small-project remodelers (both medium-project remodelers and handymen could perform some of these projects as well). It's simply that these projects routinely fall within the sweet spot in which small-project remodelers operate.

Sizing Traditional Remodelers

If you recall, a few pages ago I used typical project size to break traditional remodelers into large, medium, and small groupings.

So what exactly is their typical project size? Aren't all projects different and all sizes unique? Yes, that's correct. But when you take all their projects together, they tend to excel at one project size. That's what we are interested in determining. We don't mind that they've done a few really small projects and one or two large ones. We want their average project to be the same size as your project. Then we'll know they are essentially experts at your size project.

So how can you determine the average project size of a traditional remodeling company?

Of course, you could call and ask, "What is your typical project size?" But if you get an answer, it's likely to be misleading. Contractors always want you to think they are bigger than they are (especially if they don't already know your project type or budget). So you cannot depend on the accuracy of the answer to this question.

Instead, I'll give you two questions that the company *will* answer. And those two answers let you determine their typical project size. Why will they answer these two questions honestly? Because these two questions give them an opportunity to brag! And remodelers love to brag.

Questions:
1. How many projects do you perform in a typical year?
2. What is your typical yearly revenue?

Once you know their annual dollar volume and their average number of projects per year, simple division tells you their average project size.

Selecting the "Right" Remodelers

Your one goal here is to match your project to the ideal remodeling contractor.

To choose the right remodeler for your kitchen project, you must commit to only interviewing the best candidates for the job: you can't get the right results if you select the wrong remodeler.

So out of the vast selection of all traditional remodelers that might be able to help you, you first need to make a small list of prequalified companies to interview. How you do that is rather simple, and yet the vast majority of homeowners make huge mistakes at this very point in the process.

Regardless of how you find them (Google, Angie, recommendations, etc.), you prequalify interview candidates by making sure they pass a simple, two-part test.

To get onto your interview list, remodelers must meet these two qualifications:
1) They must have massive experience with your project type (kitchens).
2) They must have an average project size very similar to your project budget.

Let's look at these two things in more depth.

Kitchen Specialists

You always want to hire a company that has performed and will continue to perform the same project you want to do (kitchens). Why? Because they will be the most accurate in pricing and constructing their projects. They also know how to avoid most errors inherent in kitchen remodeling because they face them all the time. That kind of expertise saves you time, money, and grief, especially compared to hiring the wrong remodeler.

Don't worry that your project is redundant or that it could fail to challenge your chosen remodeler. It absolutely *is* redundant, and it likely will not challenge them!

Any remodeler with a long history of successful kitchen projects will still be thrilled to perform one for you. Furthermore, the best companies already have a hundred similar projects to their credit. They probably got into the remodeling business to do precisely that! Rest easy knowing that they are perfectly prepared to take on your project.

So look for companies that did about 50 percent (or more) kitchens during the past two years. If they did mostly basements, or maybe roofing and siding… **pass** on them. You want only folks who are well versed in kitchens, and whose website and photo book is full of kitchen projects that they designed and built.

Never give a remodeler their first big chance to do a high-quality kitchen. Be selfish and be safe… find remodelers who are already kitchen experts, and use them to get the best results.

Average Project Matches Your Budget

A few pages back we discussed how to differentiate between traditional remodelers using their averate (or typical) project size. Feel free to back up a few pages and read that again if you are not clear how to determine their average project size.

Ideally, you want the average project size of the remodelers you interview and hire to be well-aligned with your budget.

Always avoid contractors with a smaller typical project size than yours. This becomes even more critical the larger your project and budget is. It's always better to hire a costlier specialist than to give a too-small company with less experience a project above their ordinary level. As I mentioned a few moments ago, your job should not provide a remodeler with new on-the-job learning opportunities. You should hire someone for whom your project is an everyday event that they can execute with predictable ease and success.

On the other hand, hiring a company with a slightly larger typical project size than your project budget may be to your advantage if their increased skill and expertise does not come at too-high of a price. (We'll discuss how the remodeler's company structure and overhead affect you in the next section.)

For now, remember this: there are **two separate steps** in identifying a remodeler who is an ideal candidate to interview. First, that they do a **lot** of projects of your type (kitchens). And second, that their average project size is very similar to (or slightly above) your budget.

Specialty Remodelers

Specialty remodelers are companies that choose to specialize in a specific portion of the remodeling industry. Some common specialty remodelers include:

- Kitchen & Bath Remodelers
- Deck & Screened Porch Remodelers
- Basement Remodelers
- Landscape & Hardscape Design and Remodeling
- Prefabricated Sunroom Remodelers
- Closet & Storage Specialists
- Cabinet & Casework Specialists

Bear in mind that these remodelers are real remodeling companies that perform whole projects—it's just that they choose to perform just one type of project over and over as real specialists.

The only specialty remodelers in the list that we are interested in are the **kitchen & bath specialists.**

Back on the final page of the design-build remodeler chapter I said this:

> "There's one more professional design and construction combination yet to come that is right for many typical kitchen projects".

What I was referring to was the kitchen & bath specialty remodeler. Now you have the opportunity to get expert design, high-quality construction, and you get to save money… all by using this remodeler type for your kitchen.

Don't be confused by stores that sell appliances, cabinets, or other kitchen parts. If the sign or the company name includes *appliances* or *cabinets* those are *not* specialty remodelers. They are essentially kitchen product retailers. They often muddy the waters by offering "installation" or "construction by licensed and certified installers."

If you've been to a retailer that sells cabinets, you've already seen this. For example Home Depot or Lowes. These big-box stores are home-improvement retail giants. They do sell cabinets, tops, and appliances. They also offer kitchen "design" and have licensed or approved companies install or construct your new kitchen. But they *are not* specialty remodelers.

Kitchen and bath remodelers are private remodeling companies that may or may not have kitchen and bath showrooms and certified kitchen designers, but they are remodelers first. They remodel kitchens and baths, usually with a staff of full-time employees who are expert kitchen and bath carpenters and technicians. Think of them as standalone kitchen/bath design-build remodelers.

While they almost never have architects, they typically don't need them since they only design and build kitchens and bathrooms. This means they know their projects inside and out, and offer you great value since that is precisely what you need. Many such firms have a certified kitchen designer on staff. So you really get everything you need in terms of kitchen planning and implementation under one roof.

Almost all of them also sell cabinets and tops as part of their services (including fabrication and installation). But they know all about the myriad details in kitchens, and they handle them all—like electric, plumbing, flooring, tile, etc. You'll get thorough design help, help with selection of the right appliances, tops, backsplashes, vent hoods, lighting and more.

They may or may not do room size alterations (for kitchens needing additions or wall removal to combine interior spaces). That set of options varies based on each shop—so if your project requires structural changes or enlargement, just ask the kitchen & bath remodelers you track down.

You may also want to find a company with an NKBA certified kitchen designer on staff. Then you get a truly specialized kitchen design-build combination with lower overhead and lower costs than their traditional design-build counterparts.

Since they are still remodeling companies, they will obviously need to be licensed (based on your state/jurisdiction requirements) and be fully insured, just like any remodeler. Make sure any firms you consider still meet the basic qualifications that I recommend for all remodelers.

Hiring a kitchen and bath specialty remodeler could provide the best combination of expert advice or design, specific knowledge about their specialty, and lower overhead costs.

My one caution is this: in some cases, these companies have rigid relationships with specific brands or suppliers of materials. So visit with them and determine which cabinet lines, appliances, and tops they may limit you to using. Check it out in advance so that you are happy with your options. Do this **before you sign** or make any type of commitment.

Single-Line Remodelers

Single-line remodelers are companies that provide one service only. You hire them directly to do their "thing" for you. Essentially, they are a single-product subcontractor to you, the public.

Some of the services provided by single-line providers include:

- Gutter & gutter cover contractors
- Siding contractors
- Roofing contractors
- Replacement window & door contractors
- Painters
- Flooring/carpet contractors
- Granite/countertop contractors
- Basement waterproofing contractors

Essentially, these providers do only their one specialty service. Their efforts are so narrow and specialized that they cannot provide you with a "complete" project.

So while you might use a countertop vendor to make and install your new stone tops, or hire an excellent painter to paint your new project, they cannot perform your entire project.

As a result, they cannot be considered as a primary remodeler for your kitchen.

Handymen

It is important to explain the distinction between handymen and small traditional remodelers. It's a simple duration and complexity-based difference.

Handymen typically specialize in repairs and short-duration projects that require just a few hours, or at most a few days to complete. They perform tasks that you cannot perform yourself (whether that's due to lack of skills or lack of time).

Think of handymen as *honey-do-list* specialists and you won't be far off.

Projects around the house that you might call a handyman for include the following:

- All types of small physical repairs to the home
- Honey-do-list items of all kinds
- Minor drywall work or repairs
- Painting touch-ups, small paint jobs
- Installing a new door or storm door
- Changing locks or door hardware
- Adding or replacing skylights

Just remember, if you live in a jurisdiction with licensing or registration of remodeling contractors, please be certain that any handyman you hire is in compliance.

It is also important to know that when working with handymen, problems with precise clarity of the scope of work are very common. To avoid these, you should prepare a clear Project Packet, and also insist on a written or typed scope of work along with the contract you sign. Never accept verbal prices without documentation. Always work with a contract so you have that degree of protection.

And just to put a period on handymen, they are not a remodeler type you should ever consider for a complete kitchen remodeling project.

Others

There are a handful of others who could potentially cross your mind with regard to remodeling projects.

These might include:

- Carpenters who moonlight
- Friends and neighbors
- Family members
- Friends of friends
- You

My simple advice to you in all these cases is this: don't do it.

If you want professional results and the value that comes with them, then please hire the right professional (who we have already reviewed). Simply owning a truck and a hammer, or a cell phone and business card does not make people professional remodeling contractors. So unless you're having someone make you a doghouse or birdhouse, just say no to this option.

Trust me when I say, it will cost you **far more** to start a project with the wrong person or company and then complete it with the right company than it would have to hire the very best professional the first time.

If you plan to do it yourself, prepare to take at least three times as long and spend double what you think it will cost. And remember, spouses have a limited tolerance for errors and incomplete projects.

Section 3:
CHOOSE

This section helps you to identify, interview, rank, select, and sign with the ideal remodeler for your project and your personality.

Choosing the right remodeler is the single most important decision you will make throughout your kitchen remodeling journey.

This choice dramatically affects the final quality of your kitchen, your enjoyment of the experience, and your ability to remain sane and in control along the way.

It's when you identify and partner with a well-matched expert remodeler that you get the results you deserve.

So get this task correct and get ready to fall in love with your new kitchen!

Chapter 17

Find the Right Remodelers

Now that you have a complete Project Packet, the next step in your project's success is to hire the best possible remodeler. But before you can select someone to work with, you have to find, interview, and evaluate several excellent candidates.

Instead of inviting random local remodelers for interviews, you will create a short list of the most qualified remodelers, each one of whom is an ideal choice for your project.

But be careful. This is the time when many homeowners make a crucial mistake. When they realize that they don't know how to identify or evaluate remodelers, they turn to other sources to find remodeling candidates.

It's understandable. Asking Angie or Home Advisor for help is sooooo tempting. And it's super easy to ask friends and neighbors or your local community Facebook group for the names of remodelers they like.

It may be easy, but it's **wrong**. These seem like Easy Button solutions for finding remodelers. But in reality, they are lazy button solutions that will more than likely get you in trouble. What makes a remodeler a perfect fit for other people does not automatically make them right for your project.

If five neighbors with similar homes all remodeled their kitchens, I guarantee all five would be uniquely distinct. This is because each family's needs, wishes, budget, and sense of style are specific to their family. And each family should choose their remodeler based on their particular project needs, not the opinions of strangers.

Taking responsibility for selecting your remodelers can seem scary. But it's important that you do it, since you will pay for, and must live with, the results.

You would never let anyone else set your budget or make your appliance, cabinet, and countertop selections. So never let anyone else select your remodeler for you either. They'll just screw it up.

But you can get it exactly right. It's not hard, and I'll show you how.

Prescreen the Candidates

Before you look ahead toward interviewing prospective remodelers, I want you to first think back to the *remodeling mindset* you should use. **Be the Boss**.

Bosses don't sit down for interviews with every single job applicant. The applicants always get prescreened so that only the most promising candidates obtain interviews. It's the most efficient use of your time and energy.

All you need in order to prescreen remodelers is a checklist of the essential qualifications they must all meet before you invite them to an interview.

Here are the six key qualifications you'll be looking for:
- Proper remodeler type for your project
- Expert at kitchen projects
- Typical project size matches your budget
- Licensed or registered where required by law
- Minimum of seven years in business
- Fully insured

Now, let's look at each of these items in more detail so you're ready to start assessing the qualifications of your remodeler candidates.

Proper Remodeler Type

When I listed and reviewed the remodeler types, it should have been apparent that there are only a few viable options to find kitchen remodeling experts. The choices vary slightly based on the budget and complexity of your kitchen project.

The largest, most complex projects might use an architect and then bid the job with large project remodelers. Or they can consider design-build remodelers. If their project does not involve too many rooms or major additions, they can also consider kitchen and bath specialty remodelers.

Kitchen remodels without lots of rooms involved, large additions, or complex structural modifications can consider design-build remodelers, large traditional remodelers, or kitchen and bath specialty remodelers.

Smaller budget and modest kitchen remodels, staying within the current kitchen walls, would likely consider mid-size or small traditional remodelers, or perhaps a kitchen and bath specialty remodeler.

Those only planning on refacing cabinets, changing tops and flooring, and getting new appliances and new paint could consider small-size remodelers.

If you're only doing one or two things in your current kitchen (changing tops, refinishing the floor, painting, etc.), then you would look for the appropriate single-line remodeler and skip calling the larger remodeling companies altogether.

Remember, the remodeler **type** is a distinction like the specialties in medical doctors. You want to find the company that does the size and type projects you need and avoid all the others. Getting this factor right saves you much stress and wasted money. These decisions affect the quality of the design, but also the cost of the project. If you're interested in trying a remodeler one size larger than normal, try one. But focus on the best type for your scope of work.

Go back to Section 2 and read about the various Remodeler Types again if you have doubts.

Expert at Kitchens

It's essential that the kitchen remodelers you choose do numerous kitchen projects. It seems obvious and silly, but it's a big deal. You've already determined that they are the right TYPE of remodeler. Now we need to be sure they are actually kitchen experts.

Again, this is not that difficult. You're looking for someone who does 40 percent to 50 percent kitchens (or more). That means that almost every other project they perform is a kitchen remodel.

This gives you peace of mind that they know your project type inside out. They've seen it all and done it all. They will not be baffled or stumped by the routine types of problems that arise during such projects. And their staff is built specifically to remodel kitchens (and maybe baths).

You should see evidence of this on their website and their advertising. You can also make a brief, anonymous call to ask about this very topic. ("What percentage of your projects are kitchens?") Of course, you will verify this again in person when they interview.

This is a big deal. Just do it.

Typical Project Size MATCHES Your Budget

Once you have the right type of remodeler and you know they do enough kitchens to be considered an expert, you want to verify their typical project size and compare that to your budget.

If they routinely do larger projects than yours (by more than $10,000 or $15,000), then it's likely that their overhead and their final price will be a bit too high for your budget. They're used to larger budgets and built for large jobs.

If they routinely do smaller projects than your budget, by the same $10,000 to $15,000), then they specialize in smaller budget projects than yours, and yours could present some challenges to them.

But when you find a remodeler of the right type, who's a kitchen expert, and their typical project is within $15K of your budget, you've found the right remodeler to interview. They seem (for now) ideally suited to be on your short list and be interviewed for your project.

I briefly discussed how to determine a remodeler's average project size in the chapter about traditional remodelers. However, you can apply that same technique with design-build remodelers and kitchen & bath specialty remodelers. You want your project size and theirs to be very close.

Bear in mind that an average project size, by definition, is comprised of many jobs. Some will be smaller than the average and some larger than average. Some firms have more projects in their average, some have fewer. An average price is not a precise figure. That's why I suggest a $10K to $15K margin to either side of your budget.

If you choose to go beyond the $15K margin I recommend, only go higher. Get someone more experienced at larger projects. Never look for someone with less experience or whose expertise is primarily on smaller projects.

A mismatch with a company whose average project size is SMALLER than your own can be disastrous. But a mismatch with a company with a larger average project size than your own can benefit you. You'll potentially get better-skilled craftsmen with more kitchen experience, but the company's margins (and probably their total cost to you) are likely to be higher than those of a well-matched company.

Do your best to find a company with a lot of projects in the same price range as yours. They're the ideal remodeler to invite for an interview.

Licensed or Registered Only

If your state, city, or other jurisdiction licenses or registers home improvement contractors, then only ever work with those who hold valid certifications. Additionally, when there is a licensing body, you ought to visit them online (or call) to verify that the contractor you are considering is, in fact, licensed.

Never place your project and your investment at risk by using a remodeler who avoids the fundamental rules of the profession.

Find state-by-state licensing information here:
https://www.homeadvisor.com/r/state-by-state-licensing-requirements/

Experience Matters -- A Lot!

While every company and every business owner need a break to move up and try their first project of a particular size or type, I say **let them learn on someone else's dime**. Don't make your house and your kitchen a classroom for someone's on-the-job training. Choose only experienced remodelers.

Be sure everyone you consider has been in business at least seven years.

This amount of time on the job means you will avoid most of the highest-risk remodelers. It often takes a company that much time to get through the learning curve, become profitable, and get to know exactly what they're doing financially. Most of the major money hurdles that often derail remodelers are behind them after seven years.

Are They Fully Insured?

It's essential that any remodeler you consider working with be fully insured. This should include **liability insurance** and **workers' compensation** insurance.

Their liability insurance covers your home and property if an accident occurs during the performance of the remodeling project.

Their workers' compensation insurance covers jobsite accidents for their employees.

A third insurance that might come into play occasionally is yours! Your homeowner's insurance policy. What does that cover and where does the builder's insurance end and your homeowner's insurance coverage begin?

Let's take a deeper look at these three types of insurance.

Liability Insurance

General Liability Insurance is purchased by the remodeling contractor to cover damage to the property of clients (you) and others that arises during the course of doing business. Their liability insurance **protects you**, the homeowner, if something they do damages your home or your property.

Every legitimate remodeling contractor has general liability insurance.

Though claims against the liability policy of a remodeling company are quite rare, when they do occur, they are usually significant in size and scope.

Examples of liability claims could include a fire or flooding due to a mistake or negligence. If a remodeler tries to remove a tree or some tree limbs which fall and damage your home, those repair costs go against the remodeler's liability policy. If they alter the structure of your home as part of the project, and the second floor or roof sags, falls, or other damage occurs, that too is a liability issue.

Even the very safest remodeler can make a mistake or have an accident occur. And regardless of the type of damage, your homeowner's insurance does not and will not cover your remodeler's errors, so be certain that their liability policy is in place and current.

Simply ask them to present you with a policy declaration sheet, which shows the legal name of their company, its business address, and the policy size, among other information. Then verify that the policy covers the exact same company named on your proposal or contract, and also their remodeler registration or license. You should also verify that the policy is current (in date). If the policy will expire before your project is complete, insist that the remodeler provide you with a copy of the new policy when it renews. Finally, make sure the policy has at least $2 million in total coverage. You don't want to risk having the total coverage amount of the policy reached by another simultaneous claim, leaving you hanging.

Regardless of the cost of your kitchen remodel, you only want to work with companies that are properly insured just in case. It is unlikely to be needed, but it's always better to be fully covered and not need it.

Workers' Compensation Insurance

Workers' compensation insurance covers injuries to the workers of the remodeler or to the individual subs the remodeler hires to work on your project. If this policy is not in place (or current), then a worker who becomes injured on your property can sue you (and possibly get a settlement from you personally or from your homeowner's policy). Avoid such situations by asking each remodeling contractor to give you a copy of the policy at the same time you verify their liability policy.

Based on the number of employees and the business model of the company, some small remodelers and some subcontractors are NOT required to have a workers' compensation policy. If you are told this by a remodeler you are considering, please check the regulations with state remodeling or insurance officials before signing any agreement. Such waivers for workers' compensation usually cover only sole proprietors and other very small companies.

While on the subject of injury, do yourself a favor and remove obvious hazards before work begins, to eliminate any **frivolous claims against you** by an injured worker. Make sure there are no personal belongings scattered about the yard and work rooms and that there are no obvious accidents waiting to happen.

> **Pro Tip:**
>
> Always ask remodelers to provide you with three things at their interview:
> * A copy of their remodeling license (if req'd in your location), and
> * A copy of their liability insurance coverage, and
> * A copy of their workers' compensation coverage.
>
> If these are not delivered at your first meeting, make sure you receive them before you begin reviewing proposals and choosing your remodeler. If someone has not delivered their proof of insurance by then, **DO NOT USE THAT REMODELER!**

Homeowner's Insurance

While the contractor's liability policy protects you against the remodeler's negligence and accidents and their workers' compensation policy protects against jobsite injuries, neither of those protect your existing home and belongings. That responsibility falls on your homeowner's policy.

One task usually overlooked when people remodel is to contact their own homeowner's insurance agency. It is prudent to increase the total coverage amount of your policy by at least the cost of the project you are having performed. The house will absolutely go up in value as the project is completed, so your insured coverage amount should be raised to cover your home's increased value. This change might raise your premium slightly, but it could save you a tremendous amount of grief if anything goes wrong down the line.

Here's another benefit of your homeowner's policy that few understand and even fewer know about. When a project is underway, most people do not understand what materials and products are the remodeler's responsibility and which are covered by the homeowner's policy.

For instance, if the lumber piled in your driveway is stolen, who pays to replace it? What about the new cabinets and appliances stored in your garage waiting to be installed?

Here's a rule of thumb. Products that are properly attached to your home, in their final location, transfer from the remodeler's responsibility to your responsibility at that time. Up until then, all materials and products bought by the contractor are "owned" by the contractor and covered by the contractor's insurance policy. After installation, they are "owned" by you and covered by your homeowner's policy.

Pro Tip:

Contact your homeowner's insurance company and raise your policy coverage limits by the cost of your project when work begins so that you are not underinsured in case of a claim.

Insurance Verification

Insurance is something you won't be able to confirm before meeting with the remodelers for interviews. You may find information on their website about being "fully insured," which is a good start. But getting proof of insurance (declaration sheets) won't happen before you meet with them.

So when making interview appointments with the remodelers on your shortlist, ask them to prepare and deliver Liability and Worker's Comp insurance declaration sheets at the first meeting (the interview).

In the event they don't bring insurance dec sheets to the first meeting, remind them you'll need them ASAP afterward. Let them know that you will not move forward with them until proof of insurance is in hand.

And if you still have not received proof of insurance from a remodeler before their proposal arrives—don't work with them!

This is an easy request for remodelers to comply with, and it's crucial that you and they are both fully covered should anything go wrong.

Once this gets verified, concerns about negative consequences end. From here forward, it's all positive. The rest of your choices are all good, better, best.

Compile A Short List of Candidates

Regardless where you initially find them or how you identify the remodeling companies you investigate as potential interview candidates; you'll want to keep the number manageable—especially since each interview will likely take one to two hours.

This is a big reason not to invite too many companies to participate. It's much easier to invite a couple remodelers you hold in highest regard first. This limits the amount of time you must invest in interviews.

But since you should be quick to dismiss interviewees that don't live up to your expectations, or those who give you the wrong vibe, you may need a few remodelers in reserve to call on.

I suggest your short list have five to eight remodelers on it. Prequalifying that number of remodelers will take you a little time, but you only need the internet and an anonymous call or two to the remodeler's offices to get it done.

If at any time, for any reason, you learn that a particular company fails to meet every requirement on your checklist (or they don't treat you like gold), just delete them and check out the next one. There are so many qualified remodelers out there that are hoping to work with you, that you should never settle for anyone that fails to measure up!

Remember, you're building a team. You're looking for a remodeler that complements your needs, communicates comfortably with you, and is a total professional with their work.

Once your short list is filled with excellent remodelers, you're assured of working with an ideal firm that truly fits your project and your personality.

If you initially prefer a couple remodelers from the short list, list them first. This might be where their grade on Angie's List or the referral from a neighbor comes into play. If things work out beautifully, you only need to meet two, three, or four companies. So if you have favorites, call on them first.

With a finished short list of interviewees who meet your prescreening criteria, and with a complete Project Packet that's ready to go, it's finally time to set up those interviews.

Contact the top few companies on your list of vetted remodelers and ask them to set appointments to meet with you and discuss your project. Again, remember the time commitment, and only ask two or three (or four at most) to interview initially.

That's how you prequalify and create your short list of top remodelers before you even set up the first interview!

Interviewing Design-Build Remodelers

Remember, in a design-build situation, you don't get the proper design-build experience if you ask them to "bid" projects (if they even honor that request).

This is because DB companies typically charge an up-front design fee before their architect attempts to design a solution. So realistically, you need to partner with one firm and go through the design and remodeling process together with them, as a unified team.

However, you should still meet and interview two, three, or four DB firms until you find the ideal fit of architect and remodeler with your project needs. Then saddle up and go with the best one.

Your Project Packet should be complete before you arrange to speak with them. You also pre-qualify them with your checklist and create a short list of two to four "true" DB firms (who use a licensed architect) before calling to request interviews.

Your goal is to meet with the architect and a representative of the DB remodeler. If they will do that at your home, that's the best situation. If not, meet them at their office. Meeting everyone involved at one time and place is always more productive. But you won't know what's available until you call and ask.

Chapter 18

Prepare to Interview

At this point, you are fully prepared to meet with your top short-listed remodelers. The goal of each interview is to explain the project you want them to design and construct and request a proposal.

Remember, each interview can easily require between one and two hours. Be sure to allot enough time so you are not rushed.

What to Anticipate

You want to come out of the interview process with one or two remodelers you would be happy to work with. That's it.

Obviously, their prequalification needs to be verified. You will also evaluate them on a number of factors including their communications, their professionalism, their design, their price, and a few more factors, which we'll cover in later chapters.

So as you enter the interview phase, pay attention to all of your communication and interaction with these job candidates. Their answers to your questions, their enthusiasm for your project, and the quality of rapport you have with them will all help you choose the remodeler with whom you will work best.

Pay attention when they ask insightful questions about your project to better understand your vision and expectations. Evaluate your overall feeling about their representative and how comfortable you'll be working with them. Ask yourself if they were really interested in YOUR opinion and your answers, or if they were listening only so they could talk about themselves once again.

It isn't uncommon for homeowners to rule out one or two of their initial interview prospects simply because the salespeople made the homeowners feel insignificant. Or perhaps the personality of their salesperson was just odd. Maybe they arrived late and were unapologetic, or perhaps they seemed impatient to be done and get going.

Sometimes you can't articulate precisely why someone impressed you or failed to impress you.

But keep this in mind: the goal of each interview is simply to decide whether you would sign an agreement with that company assuming their design and price work out well. Literally a thumbs-up or a thumbs-down decision.

If you determine during the interview that, yes, you would like to work with them if their design and price are solid—then ask them for a design and proposal, then set a date to review their presentation.

Don't waste time on candidates that you are not willing to hire.

There are many companies that would be thrilled to work with you. Discard all remodelers who leave you with any awkward or negative feelings!

PRO TIP:

Thumbs-up? Or thumbs-down?

That is the standard for any first interview with prequalified remodelers.

After you have presented and reviewed your Project Packet with your candidate, ask yourself if you would hire them today (assuming their design and price meets your approval later). Only obtain proposals from those you give a thumbs-up!

Chapter 19

The Interviews

You've scheduled the interviews with representatives from your short-listed remodelers at your home. And you've printed out copies of your Project Packet to hand to them. There's just one thing left to focus on: the initial meeting with each of your remodeler candidates.

An Interview Agenda

After basic greetings and introductions, I suggest sitting down in a comfortable location where you can present them with your Project Packet and review it with them. Definitely avoid the traditional remodeler visit where they interview you while traipsing about your home looking at the kitchen, the electric panel, and other involved areas. Choose to handle the most important business first.

Here is a simple agenda for your first meeting with each remodeler:
- Sit and introduce your project (Elevator Pitch).
- Give them a copy of your Project Packet and review it with them.
- Do your Q&A with the remodeler (example questions in next Pro Tip).
- Answer their questions about you and your project.
- Pause here and ask: "Would I hire them?"
    - ❖ **If not,** then end the interview here.
- Let them measure and photograph the kitchen.
- Request a design & proposal from them.
- Set the appointment to review their design proposal.

Asking Questions

It puts my students at ease when I suggest sample questions for the interviewees. I'm certain many of the ideas are ones you would figure out yourself after a few minutes of thought (let alone a month or two…). But for your convenience, here are some questions that will help you verify a lot of information from the checklist and also give you some good insight into their business.

Comments [inside the brackets] are my commentary to help you clarify the question/answer.

Obviously, you should add your own questions about anything important based on your Project Packet, or about how they handle design, the contract, the construction, and the customer during a typical remodel.

PRO TIP:

What questions should you ask your remodeler candidates?
Start with these:
* *Please provide me with proof of insurance [liability + workers' comp].*
* *Please provide three or four referrals with similar size projects.*
* *Please arrange a jobsite visit [with a current client].*
* *How much total revenue do you make in a typical year?* [1]
* *How many jobs do you perform in a typical year?* [1]
* *How many jobs do you run at the same time?*
* *Do you use employees or subcontracted crews?*
* *Which subs would you use for a project like mine?*
* *What hours and days do you work?*
* *How long will it be between signing a contract to starting work?*
* *Have you ever been to court or arbitration? [Ask about the circumstances]*
* *Who will I communicate with during the design phase?*
* *How will we communicate during construction?*
* *Do you allow change orders?*
* *Are there administrative charges for* change orders?

Write (or record) everyone's answers to your questions for later comparison and review. It's valuable to have clarity on otherwise gray areas.

[1] These two questions are used to determine average project size.

This list also appears in Appendix 1 (with a download link)

Remember, the goal for each remodeler you interview is simply to decide if you would hire them, assuming you accept their design and price later on.

You literally assign a thumbs-up or a thumbs-down after each interview.

Once you're sure you don't want to work with someone, tell them immediately. Don't waste their time or yours. Say, "For several reasons, I don't think your company is a good fit for our project. Thank you for taking the time to meet with me." That's it. There's no need to even complete those interviews.

For those you do like (thumbs-up), complete the rest of the interview and then request a design and proposal from them.

Remodelers who prepare a design proposal for you will want to sit with you again in a week or two and present their design. Keep in mind that next visit is likely to be an additional one- to two-hour time investment.

After your Q&A session, each remodeler will obviously need to see the work areas to better understand the scope of the project. They will probably want to measure and photograph these areas too.

You should also be prepared to show them the main electrical panel and the main water supply shut-off valve for the home. If they need to see your furnace or AC equipment, they will ask. Make sure these different areas are free of major obstacles and easy to walk through.

With every company you interview, feel free to ask about the other personnel in the company and the roles they hold. Ask about who else you will interact with over the course of your project. You can also ask to meet those folks, including the owner, before making your final remodeler decision.

The final moments of your interviews are quite important too.

First, invite them to call or email if they find anything in the Project Packet that needs further clarification.

Next, it's a perfect time to do some budget research by asking, "Now that you understand what I'm asking for, and you've had a little while to consider that… What's your opinion about the proposed budget for the scope of work I have requested?"

Their gut feeling answer will be based on their experience. If they know for certain that you have asked for too much, they'll say so. If they honestly believe they can meet your budget, they'll tell you that. **Don't change anything** based on their answer—you're simply getting a feel for each remodeler's opinion of your project and your budget.

Then your final questions are about what's going to happen next. Ask them, "How long will it take you to design a solution and prepare your proposal?" and then "Let's set a date and time to meet and review your design/proposal."

Finally, if you're a detail-minded person, you might email each interviewee afterward and thank them for coming out. Let them know how excited you are about the project, and close with something like this: "I look forward to meeting with you again on (insert their date here) to review the design and price." (List the date they gave you for their return meeting.) This reinforces that meeting as a deadline and confirms your commitment to it.

Discussing Complaints

If your state has home improvement contractor licensing or registration, the licensing agency probably maintains a complaint database by consumers against remodelers. You may also find consumer complaints in places like Google or Angie's List.

If a company you are considering has a complaint against them (or they have a poor review on Angie's List or another reputable remodeling site), the first interview is your chance to ask about the circumstances of that complaint, so you can learn about how it was resolved. A single poor review or complaint is just a red flag to ask a question about, not a reason to eliminate an otherwise good candidate from consideration. However, multiple complaints or a number of poor reviews should probably rule out considering a particular company.

Be Sure To Ask!

There are no stupid questions. So just ask. No matter what it is.

We all tend to forget things, and there will be SO MUCH information, so take notes and write down the answers to your questions. You could even record the meetings if you want to review things later.

It's never the end of the world. You can always follow up any remodeler by phone call or email to ask a forgotten question, clarify a fuzzy point, or verify something you can't remember from their visit.

Make a note about each company when you finish your interview about whether they impressed you and would be a good fit, or if you feel for any reason that they should not be considered further. Don't carry an underwhelming company any further. Cut ties and select another firm to interview. You won't hurt their feelings. In fact, you're saving them and yourself a lot of wasted time. And most importantly, you eliminate the misery that comes from selecting the wrong remodeler.

There is always another excellent candidate out there to consider. Never settle for less than the best.

A Final Suggestion...

I suggest that you obtain from two to four proposals. You can, of course, get more if you are willing to invest the extra time to vet and interview more companies.

Once your contractors finalize their design solutions, you should expect their proposal rather promptly afterward. Each time a remodeler returns to their office to update their design, ask them when they will have the next design and proposal ready. You never want to be waiting and wondering. Always try to set the next appointment before they leave your home. When they give you dates and times, be sure to hold them to them.

If You Use an Architect + Remodeler

If you use an architect to prepare designs and drawings in advance, then you only need to present copies of those drawings to your bidders when they visit. You still interview them about their company, subs, workers, and other details listed above, but there will be no measuring or designing a solution. They will only need time to prepare the cost estimate and get you a proposal. The bidding process might even be arranged or handled by your architect in many cases.

As you may have noticed, the process is a little more streamlined in the architect + remodeler model. You'll simply wait to get all the bids back, and won't have to review the contractors based on the design, since your architect designed things in advance.

If You Use Design-Build

As mentioned briefly in Chapter 30 [Find the Right Remodelers] you will still hold in-depth Q&A interviews with each design-build firm you are considering. Ideally, the meetings will be in your home. At each interview you present your Packet and ask all the same construction-related questions noted previously. You will not be asking for designs and proposals from them since that would probably entail multiple design fees. However, you will ask questions as necessary to give you a full understanding of the company's philosophy and work methods, like you would with any remodeler. You can also ask about the design process, the typical durations for projects like yours, ownership of the designs and drawings, and the other things mentioned in the "Design-Build Remodeler" chapter.

Chapter 20

Using References

One of the most important steps you can take to protect your remodeling investment is to talk to multiple references for each company you consider hiring. It sounds cliché, but this process can tell you even more about how a company works with their customers than several interviews with the company representatives themselves. There is just no substitute for being able to ask questions of a former client to learn more about the contractor's treatment of both the project and the customer.

For example, imagine if you called a reference and asked these questions: "Did you like working with Company XYZ?" and "Would you use them again?" Of course, we all expect to hear these two answers: "We loved them!" and "Yes! We would call them again if we did another project!" If you receive any other answers than those, the remodeler who gave you that reference should be immediately eliminated for being stupid. Every reference should already be a raving fan of the company that gives them as a reference. So clearly, this is not the line of questioning you want to pursue.

Instead, you want to ask smart, open-ended questions that allow the homeowner to answer honestly without incriminating themselves or the contractor. Below I provide some questions that will get you excellent insight into how each of your prospective remodelers has worked with their customers. The answers will truly help you differentiate between the companies you're considering.

Questions for References

1. When something went wrong, how did they handle it? Were you contacted for your opinion and input? Was the issue resolved to your satisfaction? [Something always goes wrong, so this is a great way to gain insight into the problem-solving mindset of each remodeler. It also tells you if the company is proactive about problem solving, and how they work with the customer in such situations.]

2. Were they on-site daily? Did they keep regular hours? Did they alert you in advance if they would not be at your house for a day or two? [These questions give you a feel for the punctuality of each remodeler and the day-to-day schedule for their foreman and staff.]

3. Did they respect your home, your belongings, your yard? [You're looking for insight into whether they protected other rooms and furnishings, cared about dust and muddy footprints, didn't break things and knock over artwork, fixed ruts in the grass, and generally took care of the place as if they lived there.]

4. How easy were they to contact when you had a question or concern? By phone? Email? Text? The foreman, or the office? [It's important to know how easy it is to contact a company and whether they respond promptly and with proper concern and urgency when questions are asked or a need arises.]

5. When you asked about any changes to the project, how responsive were they to your inquiry, and were they generally receptive to mid-course changes? [Things always arise that you cannot foresee. You want to know if you are selecting a company that is willing to make a change that you want, or add or delete something from the project without hassles—assuming that you ask before it's too late for the requested change.]

6. What advice would you would give me if I decide to hire them to do a similar project for me? [Leave it open-ended and see what you can learn. If this question comes late or last, you're more likely to get an answer other than, "No, they did a great job."]

Asking each reference this same handful of questions will only require about five or ten minutes of your time. But what you will learn will be so valuable that it could sway your preference from one company to another, that you learn has a better reputation among their former customers.

Because this is such an integral step, you don't want to wing it. Have the questions written or typed out so you can take notes (or record them on your phone). The differences in the answers between companies will surprise you.

And whatever you do, please don't skip this step. It's far too important. You're about to spend tens of thousands of dollars, and the information you discover helps protect your investment. This step will truly put your mind at ease as you make the final choice of one company over another.

Think about it: you would never make any other purchase this expensive without spending all kinds of time and effort learning everything possible about the purchase. So spend a few minutes insuring that you hire a company that will make you happy, as they've done for their former clients. The half-hour it takes to call three references per remodeler is a very tiny investment with a huge payback that gives you incredible insight about your final candidates!

Chapter 21

Remodeling Proposals

Remodeling proposals should be a complete explanation of what the remodelers "propose" to do for you in exchange for the fee you will pay them.

Each proposal should include an original design that they believe meets your needs and a written proposal. The written portion should include a carefully written scope of work to be performed, the price you would pay for that scope of work (including any assumptions they used to estimate it), a list of inclusions and exclusions, and a discussion on any unique details or options.

Essentially, every written proposal should spell out what is, and is not, included in the price, plus the important things you should know about the construction-related details of your kitchen project.

Every proposal should be a **written document** that relates to one specific design.

They should all be organized, neat, thorough, and easily understood. Most remodelers want to present their proposals in person along with the designs so they can explain the nuances of their solution (compared to other remodelers' efforts) and answer any questions you may have.

Never accept prices or proposals verbally, regardless if it's done live or over the phone. Similarly, a scribbled price on paper—even company letterhead—is also a no-go. And if they send their price by email and they don't make a professional attempt to explain their ideas and price in a full proposal, then rule them out.

Remember, there are many more companies who would be thrilled to work with you on your project. Don't settle for proposals (or remodeling company reps) that are anything less than professional.

Chapter 22

The Heart of the Matter

You have made tremendous strides thus far if you have been working along with the plan of action I suggested. You've defined and refined your project's scope. You've clearly communicated the critical details of your project vision for your design and remodeling pros so they can develop a clever and appropriate solution. And you've identified, vetted, and then interviewed a number of excellent remodelers who could help make your kitchen renovation a reality.

Now we've arrived at the heart of the matter: who will you hire and why?

Choosing the right remodeler for your project, your budget, and your temperament is a big deal. So we're going to consider a number of factors when we review and rank your candidates. That's what the next few chapters will help with: evaluating candidates' proposals and ranking those you've interviewed.

Following that, when you've narrowed your search to just one or two remodelers, we'll look at how you can negotiate your best deal with them before signing your remodeling contract.

In the next few chapters I'll discuss the most important factors to consider while you are figuring out whom to choose. I'll suggest many good reasons why you might select one contractor instead of another. And I will also discuss the nine hundred-pound gorilla in the room: the price of the work.

Chapter 23

Evaluating Designs

At this point you should have interviewed all your initial remodeler candidates and received proposals from those you liked best. If you feel that you need to add one or two more proposals, just select the next few remodelers on your short list and hold a couple more interviews.

If you use an architect or a design-build remodeler, then you're working one-on-one with the architect to get the best solution possible for your budget. You don't do this design review with the remodelers, so you can skip to the next chapter.

Once you have received proposals from each of your final candidates, it's time to look them over.

The proposals should include two key elements: a design and the written proposal. This chapter is all about how to review and revise the designs. The next chapter discusses how you review of the rest of their proposals.

The typical design proposal includes some plans and/or images to help you envision their proposed solution for the new kitchen. Most remodelers now work with software that will let you see their solution in 3D, sometimes with realistic colors, lighting, and reflections. If you're a person that does not understand floor plans, don't worry about it—just tell your remodelers about it so they show you images in 3D and not in plans only.

When your remodelers visit to show you their solution (or deliver it for you to review), you want to ignore the written proposal for the time being. You want to focus solely on the design solution and evaluate how well it meets your needs and how much you like it.

You evaluate the design first because the cost and the quality of the remodeler mean nothing if the design fails to meet your needs or you don't like it. And realistically, nobody gets a design perfect in one try. So always determine if a solution will truly work for you before moving forward.

When a design addresses all your Need List items, all your planned Functions, and costs within 10 percent of your budget figure, then you can review the rest of the proposal and start evaluating and ranking that remodeler.

But if a design falls short in a critical area, you need to identify the flaws or omissions and let the remodeler know what's wrong. That information is essential for giving them a realistic chance to correct the solution. Be complete with your review of the proposed layout. Be sure it will work with the changes you suggest. Remember, you're only looking for critical problems, not things like materials or color choices, and not the specific details of the cabinets. Those all get selected or resolved down the line. For more information on the decision timeline of a kitchen project, see "Section 5: Preplanning".

Once you are able to list the overlooked items from your Need List or room functions list that were overlooked, review them all with the remodeler. They must clearly understand what needs to change in order to correct their solution.

When you are both in agreement about the necessary updates to the design, ask the remodeler when they will be ready to meet again to review the new design. Whenever possible, set the date for that meeting.

You certainly don't want to drag things out and make too many updates, and neither does the remodeler. So if you don't get a good solution the first time and a great solution the second time, it's probably time to say goodbye to that candidate. With the information you supplied in the Packet plus your first design review, their design should be spot-on after one revision. It should only take a couple tweaks of details to make it a fabulous solution after that.

You are not looking for design perfection at this stage. You can continue to refine the final layout, details, and price with your ideal remodeler later as needed. So don't be the person that pushes each remodeler to do three or four revisions because things aren't perfect.

You want a solution you could love, from a remodeler you'd be pleased to work with. Once you agree on the scope of work, a design, and the estimated price, you've solved the big issues, and you'll be able to work out the rest of the details pretty easily.

That's how you review the designs presented by your remodelers. You need the design to be really good or even excellent before accepting it.

About Their Price...

Before explaining how to review and rank your remodelers, there's one last note about designs. I asked you not to worry about the rest of the proposal and instead to focus on the design first. And that is all true.

But understand this about their estimated prices. You will need to glance at the price, not to compare it to the prices from the other remodelers, but to determine if it fits within your budget.

You need to be sure their different designs work and their prices are no more than 10 percent above your budget figure before you start ranking and selecting your final remodeler. To make things simple, prices more than 10 percent over budget have almost no chance of hitting the budget. There's no way to take more than 10 percent of the cost out of a design and still have a high-quality solution afterwards.

If they miss the budget with the first design, just be upfront with them and say, "This solution is too expensive for my budget. I gave you the amount I have available for the project, and your price is too far above it. Do you think you can update the design so it still works and the price is in line with my budget?"

By applying some cost saving strategies (see "Section 4: Saving Money"), and with careful material selections, you can bring a price down 5 to 10 percent, but no more. If they cannot hit your budget with their first or second design, you need to select someone else.

A great design isn't great if it exceeds your budget. In fact, it's a failure. So unless you decide you are willing to expand the budget for an awesome design, you need to challenge them to produce a design that works and meets your budget.

If your kitchen is part of a larger project, it will take more meetings to finalize those designs since there are many more details in the additional areas. But these same principles hold: the cost for each design revision should remain within 10 percent of the budget.

Know Yourself

If you are a person that simply can't understand floor plans, you must make that clear to your remodelers. It's not a flaw or a failing on your part. But it's essential that you completely understand what they are proposing for your kitchen. Never, ever say you understand something if you don't. Ask them to explain it again in a new way or show you examples so you actually get it.

3D views really help with this in most cases. If you don't understand the 3D views and images, they can sometimes make short walk-through videos showing how a design will look upon completion.

So know yourself. If you have trouble "seeing" the designs, you may need a partner to lean on who can grasp the proposed look. Never take the remodeler's word for what works for you if you can't be sure for yourself.

Resist the Temptation to Change

It can be difficult to stick with your initial ideas when you see multiple fancy designs and get lots of different prices. It can be tempting to go in another direction or try new ideas. Don't.

Changing your mind while you're preparing your Packet and shortlisting your remodelers costs you nothing but time. But **now** you are engaged with several professionals, and taking undue advantage of their time and effort is unwise.

Avoid changing your mind (and your Project Packet). Changing your mind or altering the project scope this late in the process is not just costly, but it means that **every** remodeler will need to change their design and proposal to include the new option.

Late changes can chase away good remodelers who fear that you can't make a decision and stick with it. This can also piss off your other remodelers. You don't want them changing their minds late in the process, so don't you do it either. Otherwise, everyone will have wasted their time chasing nothing.

So if someone proposes a nifty little idea that that you love, file it away in your mind. You can even have them give you an optional price for the feature. Bring it up later with the remodeler you ultimately choose. At that time, you can both explore the idea and its cost implications and see if it fits in the budget.

That's how you work with remodeling partners. Be open and honest with them at all times, so they can be open and honest with you. It's what you both deserve.

Once You Like the Design…

After you are happy with their design, here are some specific items you want them to include in their next (or final) proposal. Ask them to specifically include these five items:

- Their written description of the full scope of work
- A bulleted list of items added and omitted from the last proposal
- An itemized list of all allowances that are included in the price
- An itemized list of any owner-supplied items and services
- An itemized list of anything **not** included but necessary for the job

If each remodeler includes these things in their proposal, you will be better able to compare prices, making your final decision much simpler.

Critical Remodeling Mistake #3

Never choose your remodeler based on the lowest price!

There is only one scenario when this could possibly work out OK. If you select three or more *fabulous* remodelers with *remarkable reputations* and *perfect track records*, and they are all the *ideal type and size* for your project, and then if *all three prices are within 10%* of one another—then you can select the low-cost company. Otherwise toss out the low-price option.

The risks you face by choosing the low-price are not worth the minute savings you gain over the correctly priced proposal.

You get what you pay for. Protect your investment, your home, and your family by hiring the best company.

Cheap contractors are not the right way to save money. (See Section 4)

Chapter 24

Evaluating Prices

With regard to evaluating your remodeler prices, my advice is this: don't use price as the key factor when deciding which remodeler to hire. I know that sounds ridiculous, but hiring a remodeler based on price is a critical mistake made by far too many homeowners.

Shady and low-quality remodelers often underprice projects knowing that once they are hired, they hold your wallet in their hands and can make back the difference and more. Don't be held hostage. Instead, make your choice of remodeler based on factors other than price.

Price is obviously an important factor, but once a design is within budget, price is just one of the seven factors you use to evaluate and rank your remodelers.

About Estimated Prices

Let's discuss how you assess the estimated prices from your remodelers.

The more detailed and complete a design is, the more accurate it's estimated price can be. But since you have not yet shopped for appliances, cabinets, countertops, flooring, and other key materials, a large portion of the "price" for each design is still tentative.

For instance, your remodelers don't know if you'll choose to spend $9,000 on new stock kitchen cabinets, or $24,000 on custom cabinets, so they have to guess. They can't predict if you'll get a group A granite top or a premium quartz countertop, so once again, they have to guess. Likewise, they don't know if the floor you'll like be flamed granite tile with radiant heat or 2 ¼" oak flooring. Another guess.

The combined price difference between these three material choices would exceed $25,000. When you add the remodeler's markup (overhead + profit) on top of that, the difference could exceed $40,000! **Nobody** will voluntarily select a remodeler that is $40,000 higher than another for a typical kitchen! The higher-priced remodeler may have assumed there would be higher-quality (higher-priced) materials used than the frugal remodeler, who assumed economy selections that resulted in the lower price.

When you get three designs from three similar remodelers, you expect three similar prices. It's logical. So you would have absolutely no idea why the prices turned out so different in a case like this, or what could be done about it.

This freaks out consumers. They see huge price differences in remodeling proposals and can't understand how well-respected remodelers could price the same project so much higher or lower than one another.

The way to control this type of price disparity is to use allowances. If you recall, we ended the last chapter with five requests for your remodelers to include in their proposals. One of those was to declare all their allowances.

Each remodeler "allows" a different amount of money in their estimate for purchasing the key items and materials. By asking them to declare how many dollars they included in their proposal for cabinets, countertops, flooring, etc., you can see who allowed a little and who allowed a lot.

When you know the allowances in each remodeler's price, you can eliminate the single biggest (normally) hidden variable between companies. With a pencil and a calculator, you can normalize their bid prices. The difference between the adjusted prices then reflects the various markups (profit and overhead) and business model efficiencies of your bidders.

This is possible only when you take back control of the handful of costly materials by using allowances.

I've included a technique in the "Saving Money" section about using allowances. Check that out for more detail.

Comparing Prices

Let's be honest, people always rank the "bid" prices they receive. And if you insist that your candidates declare the allowances they include, you, too, can start comparing prices.

But you should consider a few other things along with each price. Was each price under (or at least near) your budget figure? If it went above your budget figure, did they offer you alternatives and options that would result in a more on-target price?

There is no way to know with absolute certainty that any price is accurate, complete, or fair. And believe it or not, remodelers make a lot of mistakes in estimating, sometimes very simple math errors. What you are looking for when considering several proposed costs are a few that are closely grouped. As a rule, you might like to see prices be within 10–12 percent of one another (within $5,000–$6,000 for a $50,000 project, or within ~$10,000–$12,000 for a $100,000 project). In such cases, I would consider those prices "equivalent."

You may have heard folks say you need to get three prices to be sure you get a fair offer. I believe that's wrong. If you really, truly want to shop based on price (which I don't advise), you probably need five prices from equivalent remodelers. My logic is this: the highest price of the five bids should be discarded. While I truly believe that "you get what you pay for" and "quality costs money," you will never choose the highest price of five or more if they are truly equivalent remodelers. Also, the high price is high for a reason. If a company is very busy and doesn't need another project at that exact moment, they will raise their profit margin (and price) so they are handsomely paid if they get your project. Another common reason for a too-high price is an estimating mistake. So don't entertain the highest bid unless you've fallen in love with their design and professionalism.

Just as I said that the highest price is high for a reason, there are also reasons that the lowest price is low. The most common reason for a too-low price (one greater than the ~10 percent difference I mentioned) is an estimation mistake. And you **do not** want to be halfway in when your remodeler realizes that they will lose money on your project due to their error. Work could slow down or stop, and they could redirect their best efforts toward more profitable projects to keep cash flowing. The second most common reason for a too-low price is an intentionally low bid to win the project. This happens when they are hurting financially and are desperate for funds. Being contractually bound to a low bidder places you in a precarious position. The phrases "over a barrel" and "between a rock and a hard place" come to my mind. Do yourself a favor and throw out the lowest price.

After eliminating the high and low prices, you should find that two (or all three) remaining prices are reasonably close (within about 10 percent of one another). This is a great indication of the most accurate price range for your project.

Chapter 25

Other Ranking Criteria

We've already looked at using remodeler references, as well as how to evaluate their proposed designs and prices.

The remaining four categories used to rank remodelers are their qualifications, their professionalism, their overall proposal, and your personal preference.

Together these factors give you a unique way to evaluate and rank the different remodelers in a way that is as objective as possible.

Qualifications

Each contractor that you interviewed was prequalified to meet certain standards. Some of those were that they performed at least 40 to 50 percent kitchen projects (were kitchen experts), that their typical project size is within 10 percent of your project budget, that they are the right type of remodeler for your needs, that they have been in business at least seven years, and that they are fully insured.

For those who live in jurisdictions that license or register remodelers, 100 percent of those interviewed should have been properly licensed or registered.

As you review each remodeler and think only on these characteristics (their qualifications), some will stand out as better qualified, and one or two as lesser qualified.

That's all we're looking at with regards to qualifications, who's the most qualified to perform your kitchen remodel, and who has slightly less qualifications. No judgement since they all met minimum standards, but some are simply more qualified.

Professionalism

In this case you should look back at each of your interview candidates and ask which one (or ones) presented themselves most professionally?

Their literature, their website, cars and trucks, personnel, offices, and paperwork ought to be professional in appearance and practice. They should have great pride in their stature in the community and industry, have their insurance and registration (or license) in order, be properly insured, and have excellent communications with you. Every contact with them should leave you feeling confident in their ability to help you through this process and perform your project successfully.

In this industry especially, punctuality is critical, and often lacking. Their respect for your time should be evident by their timely attendance at all meetings, timely returns of calls and emails, and meeting all self-selected deadlines.

When companies take care and pride in their appearance to the customer and the public, in all facets of their business and show respect, then they are acting as true professional remodelers ought to act.

Proposal Quality

Was their proposal handwritten on a napkin or a three-ring notebook page, or typed and professionally presented on letterhead? Did they make a phone call with their "price," or did they take the time to clearly write out the scope of work, the cost of that work, and any options and extras that were discussed with you?

Was the proposal neat? Was it clearly written in words and terms you understood so that both you and the remodeler could have a clear understanding of the proposed work to be performed? Did it look clean and professional?

The job of the proposal is to clearly define the entire scope of work—what is and what is not included. There should be no ambiguity. It needs to be totally clear and understood by both you and the remodeler. It will become part of the contract so it must be clear—black and white with no gray areas. A well-crafted, clear proposal is a significant indication of a detail-minded, customer-oriented professional.

Preference

This one is as simple as it sounds. Which company impressed you more? With whom did you have a very easy rapport? Who was able to see your vision clearly and help you refine it? Whose ideas thrilled you most? Which company best offers you a combination of value and cost? Who was able to educate you about their solution and the way they would approach the process?

While it would be nice to be totally objective when choosing a kitchen remodeler, your opinion and comfort level does matter. It's not the only issue upon which the hire is made. You don't "follow your gut" and hire the one that "felt best."

But we acknowledge that who you like and prefer to work with makes a difference. I trust that nobody you don't like and do not want to work with made the cut! But you probably have a preference, and this category lets you voice that as one of the factors on which to choose your ideal remodeler.

Chapter 26

Ranking Your Remodelers

The hard work of finding, vetting, interviewing, and evaluating remodelers is done.

While it would seem that making your decision about which one or two remodelers you should negotiate with and sign a contract with would be the most difficult choice, that's not true.

Using my Remodeler Scorecard (below) lets you think about your remodeler one facet or topic at a time and record those ranks.

REMODELER SCORECARD								
Remodeler Name	Qualifications	Professionalism	Design	Proposal	Preference	Price	References	TOTAL SCORE
A								
B								
C								
D								
E								

How the Scorecard Works

List the two to five remodelers you are evaluating in the Remodeler Name column. Then you see that the evaluation attributes we reviewed in the last few chapters each have a column on the scorecard.

Qualifications Column

Starting with Qualifications column, assign the score of 10 to the one remodeler that had the best possible qualifications of those you interviewed. Then assign the score of 9 to the second-best remodeler in terms of their qualifications. Assign the score of 8 to the third-best-qualified remodeler. Assign the score of 7 to the fourth-best-qualified remodeler. Assign the score of 6 to the fifth-best-qualified remodeler.

If you think remodeler C, D, and E were all similarly qualified, then give them all the third-best score of 8 points.

But the top score of 10 can only go to one remodeler, the one that was best of all in the Qualifications category.

Professionalism Column

In the Professionalism column, assign the score of 10 to the one remodeler that presented themselves in the most professional manner. Review the discussion of a professional remodeler if you have any doubts. Then assign the score of 9 to the second-best remodeler in terms of their professionalism. Assign the scores of 8, 7, and 6 to the third-, fourth-, and fifth-best remodelers (in order) based on your impression of their professionalism.

If you think to or three remodelers were identical in their professionalism, then give them the same score.

But the top score of 10 can only go to one remodeler, the one that was best of all in the Professionalism category.

Design Column

In the Design column, assign the score of 10 to the one remodeler that presented you with the most innovative, most enjoyable design that truly met your needs. Review the chapter on evaluating designs if you need a refresher on the topic. Then assign the score of 9 (or lower) to the second-best design based on the score of 10 for the best design. Assign scores of 8, 7, and 6 (or lower) to the third-, fourth-, and fifth-best remodeler's designs based on the score that you just assigned to the second-best design.

If you think two of the designs (#2 through #5) are identical in rank, assign them the same score, and drop a point or two for the next-lower-ranked design.

But the top score of 10 can only go to one remodeler, and that should be the one that gave you the very best design.

Proposal Column

In the Proposal column, assign the score of 10 to the one remodeler that presented you with the best overall proposal. It was neat, professional, clear and concise, thorough, understandable and the way you wish all the other designs had been done.

Then assign the score of 9 (or lower) to the second-best proposal. Assign the scores of 8, 7, and 6 (or lower) to the remaining proposals as you compare them to the best and second-best ones.

Preference Column

In this column, your personal opinion about each company is how you rank them. Assign the score of 10 to the one remodeler that you would most like to work with based on your experience during interviews and design iterations.

Assign the score of 9 (or lower) to the company you liked second-best. Then assign the next lower scores to the other three remodelers in the order you would prefer to work with them.

Price Column

In the Price column, assign the score of 10 to the remodeler that presented you the best price. Assign a score of 9 to the next best price. Do it again for the other remodelers you are ranking.

However, if anyone's price was significantly above your budget, drop their ranking to 5 or below. You cannot reward a company that failed to meet your basic needs and deliver an on-budget solution with a high score.

References Column

In the References column, assign the score of 10 to the one remodeler whose references gave the best information and clear understanding of that remodeler's commitment to excellence. They have the best communications, are the most honest, are present daily, answer phone calls, solve problems, and take care of the customer's property.

Assign 9 or lower scores to the remaining remodelers based on the feedback you received talking to their references.

Total the Scores

After filling in all seven columns of rankings, simply total the scores for each remodeler on their row in the right-hand column, Total Score. Do this for each remodeler so you can review their totals.

Reading the Results

The remodelers with the weaker scores (regardless of how they got them) will now fall well behind the leader(s) in Total Score.

Typically one, sometimes two remodelers have a similarly high score. Those one, or two remodelers are the only ones you should pursue with your negotiations.

The top company, or one of the two top companies, is the ideal remodeler for your kitchen project.

REMODELER SCORECARD								
Remodeler Name	Qualifcations	Professionalism	Design	Proposal	Preference	Price	References	TOTAL SCORE
A AAA Improvements	8	8	9	9	9	9	9	61
B Ace Home Services	9	9	7	8	7	7	7	54
C Maple Design-Build	10	9	10	9	9	8	10	65
D River Remodeling	9	8	8	8	8	10	9	60
E Stone Contracting	9	10	9	10	10	9	9	66

In the sample scorecard above, two remodelers (C and E) clearly have the best scores. I would carry **both** of them to the negotiations stage to see which one I could get the very best deal from.

But at this point the Scorecard shows that I can move ahead with Maple Design-Build or Stone Contracting. Both had higher total scores than any of the others, and both rated highest in numerous ranking categories as well.

If you plan on taking two remodelers to negotiations, then there is more good information you can glean from the Scorecard.

Maple Design-Build had the best qualifications and design, but fell down a few notches on price.

Stone Contracting had a better price and was the more preferred contractor, but their design was not the favorite.

When you get to negotiations (next chapter), these pieces of information will help you decide the most advantageous technique to try with each remodeler in an effort to get your best possible deal.

Chapter 27

How (and When) to Negotiate

In the 4th section, "Saving Money," I teach several methods that will save you money and reduce the total cost of your project. Those savings techniques get implemented as you begin meeting contractors and starting interviews (before designs, proposals, and prices are even in play). But all of those techniques are geared toward saving money. They are not ***negotiating***.

Of course you can save money when you negotiate. But if you hope to knock $10,000 or $20,000 off your price, you can't wait until it's time to sign a contract. Then you're too late and it won't happen. Your biggest potential savings (price reductions) come from applying the "Saving Money" techniques, not your final price negotiation.

Remodeling negotiation is not a "win at all costs" effort. You are not trying to beat the remodeler. Remember, you're building a team that is responsible for constructing your dream kitchen. You want the agreement with your remodeler to be good for both of you… a win-win scenario.

You win when you get the best possible deal. You can either get a better total price, or more project for the proposed price.

The remodeler wins when they get you to sign a contract and they keep as much profit as possible.

Win-win techniques like the ones I am about to share
- Get "yes" answers,
- Are respectful of both parties, and
- Save you thousands or improve your project.

By now, you should be done ranking your remodelers and have one (or at most two) contractors that you would like to negotiate with.

This is the one and only time in the process where you should negotiate.

In my experience, you get one opportunity to ask each contractor for a better deal or a price concession. The time to do it is after you've narrowed your selection down to one or two choices. Ask sooner, and they will all ignore you. Ask later, and they'll say no.

All the negotiation techniques I teach are meant to be used after all interviews are done, and before you visit with your favorite contractor(s) to talk about contracts.

Before we talk about the mechanics of remodeling negotiation, you need to understand how remodelers arrive at their price.

A remodeler's total price is comprised of their hard job costs (labor, subs, and materials), overhead (costs of non-project-related business expenses like rent, utilities, cars and trucks, office staff, etc.), and profit.

Most remodelers aim for about 10 to 15 percent profit (the money remaining after paying their costs and overhead). If they have estimated your project accurately and perform the project efficiently, they will make closer to 15 percent profit. If they have made errors in their estimate or if they produce the project inefficiently, then their profits are reduced, perhaps significantly. (I go into additional detail about remodeling pricing [costs + overhead + profit] and how their company structure effects their prices in the Saving Money section of the book, because understanding overhead actually leads to your biggest cost savings potential).

The reason I mention profit margins is that most homeowners ask for price concessions that are much too large, meaning too much of a "discount." For example, if your price from a remodeler is $50,000 and you ask them to sign for $45,000, you have asked them to give up $5,000, or about two-thirds of their potential profit (assuming they priced and produce the job correctly). Honest companies, who price their work fairly, absolutely cannot eliminate two-thirds of their profit just because you asked them to lower their price.

As a rule of thumb, most substantial price reductions from honest contractors require a reduction in the scope of work, or the use of lower allowances, or other such trade-offs. If you think it's unfair that they won't make a larger price reduction, think how you would react if they asked you to agree to a smaller scope of work just before signing the contract at full price!

I imagine you're thinking, "Jim, you're teaching us to negotiate, but you're telling us there's no wiggle room in the price?" That's right. I'm explaining why a straight price reduction is *not* the best way to approach your one and only negotiation. You can usually get one, but it may be smaller than you hope.

I explain three different negotiation techniques that are all very likely to be successful if you follow the guidelines. These methods all result in either a better price, or a better total value for you, without reducing the scope or the quality of your project.

The Round-Down

When you have just one remodeler you wish to work with, this is the best technique if you prefer a straight price reduction.

You will be requesting them to "round down" their price to a nice big round number. You are trying to lower the cost without changing the defined scope of work.

The Pitch

You contact them in person and tell them the following: "I'm prepared to sign a contract with you, using the current scope of work, if the contract price is $XX,XXX."

When you present your request like this, you are not inviting additional negotiation; it's more of a take-it-or-leave-it request.

The Logic

Remember, their profit margin is about 10 to 15 percent of the total price. So after you figure out what that is in dollars, you want to ask for about one-third to one-half of their profit. The interesting factor in this method is selecting the big round number you ask to hit with the reduction.

"Big round numbers" are those that end in 000 for large jobs and maybe 000 and 500 on small jobs. On a small project, you might ask for a round down from $31,200 to $30,000. On a larger project, you might suggest a round down from $83,800 to $80,000.

When you respect their profit and ask for a reduction that is between 3 and 5 percent of their profit, you'll be successful in a majority of cases.

Possible Outcomes

Remember, you are naming a price. As a result, you risk losing this negotiation.

Pro Tip:

In all negotiations, the first one to name a figure loses. If you ask for $5,000 off the price or ask them to do it for $55,000 instead of $60,000, the obvious response they make is to cut your suggested difference in half. So don't suggest the solution to them; instead just tell them you want an improved offer in exchange for signing with them as your contractor.

In these three techniques, you're in a take-it-or-leave-it situation. This is a one-time opportunity, and if you're turned down, it's wise to predecide if you will accept the original price or go find another contractor.

It is still possible to get a counter-offer that's lower than the initial price but not as low as what you requested.

Considering that kitchen projects are often $35,000 and up, this technique still saves you from $1,000 to $2,000 on modest projects, and more on larger ones.

Price Reduction w/ a Twist

This technique takes advantage of a lower price to get a price concession from your preferred remodeler, whose price is higher. When your second-choice contractor has the lower price, this method is ideal. If your first-choice turns down your request (or it's just not as much of a discount as you expect), you can happily go negotiate and then sign with your second-choice remodeler.

You **are not** trying to get the two remodelers into a bidding war. And remember, you only get to negotiate once with each remodeler. So think carefully before starting this negotiation.

The Pitch

Speaking directly to your preferred, higher-priced contractor in person or by phone only (no texts or emails), explain that you prefer to work with them above the other companies you interviewed. However, a second contractor with whom you are willing to sign, has offered a lower price. Then you make this simple request: **"Their lower price is $XX,XXX. If you can do something to bring your price more in line with theirs, then I'm prepared to sign with you instead."**

Feel free to give the real lower cost from the other remodeler, but **do not** reveal the other contractor's name.

The Logic

By making your request simple and open-ended (without declaring a particular final price or discount amount), you intentionally place the entire solution in their hands. Knowing that you are willing to sign with them should motivate them to suggest a very reasonable discount.

After you have made the request… shut up. You don't say another word about prices or contracts until after they respond.

Possible Outcomes

In almost every case, they will offer you a price reduction. The only question is whether the reduction is enough so you will sign with them. You have not made a specific dollar request, so the hard work is all on their end. They know they either win your job or lose your job based on their response. So they are motivated to try to make you a good offer.

Once they make a new price offer, negotiations with them are now over. In our scenario, you either agree to their lowered price and sign with your first-choice remodeler, or you go negotiate with the second-choice remodeler who already has the lower price.

So, your response is either, "Yes, I accept that offer," and you sign with your favorite, or you tell them, "I need to consider whether I can pay your price or if I need to sign with my other remodeler. I'll let you know my decision soon."

This method always gets a cost reduction from your preferred contractor. It may not be enough of a discount, but they will attempt to make their price more attractive.

Either way this plays out… you win. You either get your favored contractor at a much better price, or you get another excellent contractor at the best price (and you have not yet negotiated with them!).

Increase the Scope

You will not be shocked to hear that remodelers are much happier when you agree to pay their proposed price. But that's not negotiating, is it?

When you've gone through the steps outlined in this book, you will be fully convinced that your top-ranked remodeler is a legitimate professional. For this reason, you might not balk at their proposed price. Or maybe you're not keen to "negotiate" or haggle since you know you're cutting into their profits. But there is still a way you can benefit when you agree to pay their asking price.

During large projects and most medium ones, you discuss lots of nifty options before arriving at the final design, scope of work, and proposed price. Many of your Wish List items get omitted for purely financial reasons. Here is your chance to negotiate and get one special thing from your list put back into the project. This is the time and this is the method to get it included for free, or at a steep discount.

The Pitch

Here's how I suggest you pitch it to the remodeler of your choice: "I'm prepared to sign with you and pay your full proposal price, but I'd like you to include that (name of feature) that we discussed earlier. If you add that in at the current price, I'm ready to sign the contract."

The Logic

The reason your remodeler is likely to accept is two-fold.

First, you're prepared to sign the contract. And they don't want to lose a sale by saying no. If you've been a nuisance-free client throughout the process and they are interested in your project, they'll work with your one-and-only request for a concession.

Second, if you're asking for several hours of labor and some common materials that fit easily into the flow of work for the big project, then only the purchase of specialty items or materials actually add to their cost. In that case, they might ask you to pay a bit of the extra purchase costs, but they'll eat the labor and overhead.

As you prepare to negotiate with this technique, make sure the amount of the extra feature you ask for is not more than 10 percent of the project cost.

Possible Outcomes

When your request includes additional cabinetry, additional granite or quartz tops, additional upscale doors or windows, or other premium materials, you should be prepared for the contractor to make a counteroffer.

When I negotiated as a remodeler, I often said things like, "I'll give you the labor to install your additional skylights, if **you** pay the actual cost of the skylights," or

"That lift-top window seat would cost about $4,000 in materials and labor. I'll split that cost with you, adding only $2,000 to the price but doing the seat in the same manner we previously discussed."

A good kitchen example might be a tile backsplash. If the tile cost is modest (not a premium stone, glass, or metal), I would expect the remodeler to just say "okay". Installing a tile backsplash in your kitchen won't cost them much in time and labor, but they might ask you to supply or pay for the tile itself if it is a costly material.

Even when the resolution to your request is not free, the modest additional cost gets you more project. It's a smart way to bulk-up your project just before signing.

Only ONE OPTION Applies

Please remember, you can only try **one** of these negotiation techniques with each remodeler you might hire. You can't ask for a round-down AND an add-on. You can't ask them to cut their price to approach a lower bidder and then also ask them to round down. Because of this, you'll need to consider your situation and the relative prices from your remodelers, before you choose the negotiation method you will use.

And while it goes without saying, I will mention it anyhow: be true to your word. Don't ask for a concession using the caveat, "If you do this, I'm prepared to sign the contract" and then fail to follow through. You would immediately drop a remodeler that broke their word to you, so don't do it to them.

Chapter 28

Remodeling Contracts

As I've stated all along the way, you must always sign a contract when you remodel, if for no other reason than to protect your investment. I think we can all agree that remodeling costs are large, probably even larger than you realized. Don't risk that amount and more on a "gut feeling" or on the word of a remodeling salesperson. I'm not suggesting that all remodelers are liars and scoundrels -- far from it -- but a contract is your best protection if problems do arise.

Before I discuss the most common remodeling contract details, let me mention the two contract types that are **not** written by the contractor in cooperation with the owner: (1) standardized contracts that are written by an architect (AIA 101/107), or (2) contracts written by a bank (with bank-controlled disbursements). In these cases, the homeowner and contractor have little say about the contract terms (at least regarding the payment schedule). They simply sign the documents and become parties to the agreement. Control over the process is maintained by the contract agent (the architect or the bank), though it is possible the architect or bank will work on the draw schedule or disbursement terms directly with your contractor. If you use an architect or have a bank-controlled loan, then be sure to discuss the terms of that particular contract with your architect or banker.

My final note before we dive into contract information is that I am NOT an attorney. This is NOT legal advice. You should feel free to consult a lawyer when presented with contracts by your selected remodelers.

This chapter will familiarize you with the basics of remodeling contracts so you can scan yours and have an understanding of some of the key sections.

Typical Remodeling Contract Requirements

The following items relate to features or sections that any reasonable remodeling contract will contain. Become familiar with these, and be sure to ask your remodeler for a blank or draft contract to review **in advance** of receiving their proposal. This will give you time to read it over and discuss modifications without delaying signing when the time comes. In the event the contractor is reluctant to alter their agreement for you, I would suggest that should affect your final decision about whom to hire.

Parties to the Contract

Every legitimate contract starts by identifying all parties to the contract by name, address, and contact information (phone and email). In most cases, this includes the contractor and the homeowner. A contractor's license number should also be displayed if you reside in a jurisdiction with licensing or registration. The name of the contractor used in this section should match the name on their insurance documents and all other printed materials. If not, don't sign.

Total Price and Payment Terms

The agreed-upon total price of the contract needs to be clearly displayed. All individual payments (called *draws*) need to be clearly listed, detailing the amount due and the milestone in construction that triggers each draw payment.

In most cases, the homeowner and contractor can negotiate the size of the payments and the milestones that trigger them so that money is being paid only as progress on the project is accomplished. It is recommended that a very large initial payment (deposit) be avoided. A rule of thumb is for the deposit to be one or two times the regular payments, and the final payment to be about half the deposit amount.

In my opinion weekly or bi-weekly payments allow the homeowner to feel comfortable with the progress in construction. This also provides regular cash flow and incentive for the contractor to maintain the scheduled flow of production.

The final payment, or a portion of it, should be held back until all punch-list items are completed (punch list: a written list of the last remaining details as the project winds down that should be signed by both parties).

Dates

There are two sets of dates in every contract. Contracts are dated when they are signed by all parties involved, and this is the date of contract origination. All contracts should also include start and completion dates for the project, or a start date and project duration.

Sometimes these dates are unknown at contract signing and may appear as "within a week of the building permit being issued" or "to be determined." The duration of a project might be stated as "13 weeks" or "12 days" or "4 months." Ask your remodeler to put in terms that are most suitable for your situation.

There will usually be a disaster clause in case of strikes, wars, acts of God, etc., that allow the schedule to be expanded. If you wish your project to be completed by a particular date, that needs to be specifically included in the contract along with a penalty clause in case of failure to do so. But this must be discussed with each remodeling candidate during the initial interviews, since some may not be able to meet your fixed completion date.

The date of the contract origination often occurs on the first page with the parties and payment terms. The contract signing dates are usually on the signature pages where both parties sign and agree to the contract. The project start and end dates often appear elsewhere, not at the beginning of the contract; so be sure to look for them and verify them.

Permits and Inspections

If you live in a jurisdiction where permits and inspections are required, then you must include a clause in the contract that states the contractor is responsible for obtaining all required permits and inspections for the project.

Scope of Work and Drawings

The contract is not the only document that you should be concerned with. Any design or permit drawings and their specifications are also part of the remodeler's contract with you. The drawings and specs are separate documents, so they need to be added to the contract as *exhibits*. They should be referenced in the text of the contract as being part of the contract or agreement between parties. It is possible on smaller projects to literally type all the specifications into the contract itself. Both methods are fine. Just be sure that the exact set of drawings and specs you are agreeing to are fully referenced in your contract. In this way, everything stated and shown as part of the scope of work on the construction documents is also part of the contractual agreement between you and the remodeler.

If you already have auxiliary drawings such as from a cabinet manufacturer or supplier, those too should be specifically named and incorporated into the contract in this same manner as an exhibit of the contract.

Materials

If your project will be using very specific brands, models, materials, or colors of materials, then those should be called out. They can be written out in a section of the contract, they can appear in the project specifications, or they can appear on the project drawings. Read through the selections before signing, so that you are sure the choices you want to be included are the ones in the contract.

Warranty

Every contract should include terms of the warranty granted by the remodeler. Minimum warranty information should include the following:
- duration of the warranty period (how much time)
- any maintenance required as a condition of the warranty
- the remodeler's obligation to the homeowner during the warranty period
- the procedure a homeowner follows to obtain warranty service

Dispute Resolution

The very best dispute resolution protection you can have is to select a remodeler who honors their obligations to customers and avoids litigation and arbitration at all costs. Discussing your concerns with a caring remodeler is so much easier than fighting about a resolution. This is why it's so vitally important to call every reference to ask how problems were handled and if there were ever any misunderstandings. Then choose a contractor that has never been taken to court or arbitration. This is always your best protection.

Below I discuss the two primary dispute resolution methods used by remodelers: the courts and arbitration.

Going to Court

Courts are slow and very expensive. And even if you win your case, you'll spend lots of money, endure lots of project downtime, and become enemies with your remodeler. And don't forget that in most cases, the initial result can be appealed. The only real winners in litigation are the lawyers.

Arbitration Clause

An arbitration clause in a home improvement contract should include the following:
- The name of the organization that will conduct the arbitration
- Any mandatory fees that will be charged to the parties
- Whether the arbitrator's findings are binding

Typically, the dispute resolution clause requires a separate signature page within the contract. The requirements may vary by jurisdiction.

I favor arbitration since it is much swifter and often substantially cheaper, and if you use a group like the BBB to arbitrate disputes, they are often compassionate towards the homeowner.

Making Changes

All remodeling contracts need to explain how to change the contract. Once it is signed, it is a binding legal agreement, so altering it must be done legally. You should never take anyone's word for any changes of substance to your contract. Typically, remodeling contracts are altered by a written *change order*. A *change order* is a brief (often single-page) document that sets the scope of the change and the price change of the change. It is also signed and dated by all parties.

Changes could be for additional work, the omission of work that was in the initial agreement, or just a change to some facet of the project. Change Orders are necessary even if the change does not require the overall price to be changed.

Be certain there's a way to alter or amend the contract and that you understand how it works (whether there are administrative fees, etc.).

Section 4:
SAVING MONEY

This section explains the best assortment of cost-saving measures that I know. You may want to use one or more of these methods to help reduce the total cost of your project.

Especially for kitchen projects, these methods will allow you to save a substantial amount (with the willing cooperation of your remodeler). Total savings with these methods will exceed the savings from your final price negotiation by a large margin.

If you decide to use any of these techniques, discuss them with your remodelers when you first meet for interviews. Do not wait for final price negotiations to find out that a remodeler will not cooperate with you on these methods.

Chapter 29

Controlling Costs

Everyone wants to pay the lowest amount possible and get the best job possible.

The problem is that only an industry-savvy person can discern what is truly the least possible amount and best possible outcome in any given situation.

So I recommend that you try to spend the least amount *necessary*. You don't want to skimp on the design, the appliances, cabinets, tops, quality of your remodeler and subs, or the end results. That is why I suggest that your project goal should be to get the best kitchen possible for a fair price. Paying the "lowest price" should never even be an option.

Here is a Value Triangle. This has an important application in remodeling when we try to balance Cost, Quality, and Time.

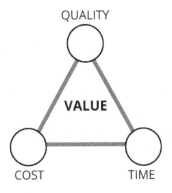

You, the homeowner control two of the nodes, and the third one is sacrificed. So which two would you choose for your project?

If you choose best cost and highest quality, the project will take forever. If you want top-quality results and the swiftest production time, then the cost will increase. And if you want an inexpensive project that's fast, the quality stinks.

I use this to illustrate that making a decision based on a single factor (cost) has ramifications that are unseen by most people. However, if you pursue great value in a kitchen, you can be satisfied.

When you acknowledge that paying a fair price in exchange for a high-quality project in a reasonable timeframe is a good thing, the possibilities for success increase.

Buying on price is the third of three critical remodeling mistakes (in addition to starting projects unprepared and choosing the wrong remodeler), and it almost always increases project stress and project failures. There is always a reason that the lowest price is low, and you don't ever want to learn what those reasons were.

So, in remodeling, the most applicable adage is, "You get what you pay for."

But it is possible for you to reduce the cost of your project by applying a few of the insider techniques in this chapter.

First, I will explain how to minimize the variability of prices from different remodelers in a bid situation. I will also explain how you can perform some tasks for yourself so the remodeler does not need to perform them for you, saving his time and your money. I will also discuss what portions of projects allow for "doing it yourself" and actually saving some money without hurting the project quality. Finally, I will show you how you can save many thousands of dollars (with the cooperation of your remodeler) when you shop for some of the key products used in your kitchen.

These techniques and suggestions will not make the companies you select give you identical prices, but their prices will be lower and more comparable. And the best part of these methods is that the quality of your kitchen will not suffer, nor will the time it takes to complete it.

Use Allowances

In mid-size and large projects, you should always try and control your costs using allowances. In simple terms, allowances are little piles of money that the remodeler will set aside within the estimated price to buy items or services used in the performance of your project. Allowances can be used for myriad items or services. Some of the most common ones for kitchen projects are:

- Cabinets
- Countertops
- Appliances
- Light fixtures
- Plumbing fixtures
- Flooring materials
- Tile
- Exterior doors & windows
- Electrician costs
- Plumber costs
- Specialty features (unique range hoods, etc.)

The simplest thing you can do to help hold your costs down and get valuable financial feedback about your remodeling candidates is to have each of them declare all the allowance figures used in your project. How will this help you? Let's take a look.

Without your input, the price each company gives you includes a different amount of funds for the purchase of the expensive, core items and services.

Some companies try to minimize those figures to keep their bottom-line cost lower and more attractive to homeowners, most of whom shop based on price. Other remodelers include much larger amounts to buy better cabinets, tops, and premium flooring so that you can select higher-quality or higher-priced items for a better end product.

But if you don't know what amounts were set aside (allowed), you would never know that the lower-priced proposal did not include enough money to purchase the items you want and that the higher-priced option easily accounted for those premium selections.

When you ask remodeling contractors to declare the allowances included in their proposed prices, you can see who allots more and who allots less for the different allowance items included. This helps you eliminate the common problems associated with low bids.

Owners who sign a low-priced contract and find out later that there wasn't enough money set aside to buy the cabinets and tops they desire, are stuck. They have no choice but to pull out the checkbook and pay those additional costs mid-project, or select low-quality products that hurt the look and performance of the kitchen. You can easily find yourself in an impossible situation if you sign a contract without having the allowance amounts declared.

When all your bidders declare the allowance amounts in their price, you can easily see the difference in allowed costs. This lets you ask, "Why are your cabinet and top allowances so low?" or "Can you show me what brand and line of cabinets that allowance will purchase?" You can also ask about the much higher allowances. This gives you a chance to learn about and manage the biggest and most important costs *before* selecting the final contractor and signing a contract.

When you use allowances, you limit the most variable expenses of the whole kitchen. Realistically, the remaining expenses should be reasonably similar across the board between your various candidates. In other words, the actual cost of materials and labor to perform the project should be quite similar from one company to the next. The same is true for their cost of subcontractors (electrician, plumber, etc.). Consider the following table.

	Townhouse Kitchen Remodel		
	Estimate 1	Estimate 2	Estimate 3
Materials and Labor	$6,610	$6,610	$6,610
Overhead & Profit	$11,047	$12,694	$14,636
Allowance Items	$13,500	$16,470	$20,000
Total Proposed Cost	$31,157	$35,774	$41,246

This table shows three estimates for a small townhouse kitchen with a very small island. The **only** significant difference in these three prices are the three different allowance levels. The cost of the cabinets, countertops, and hardwood flooring were priced at modest, average, and slightly upscale levels in the three proposals. The materials and labor costs of all three are identical.

The large variation in the total cost illustrates how dramatically a few line items change what the homeowner sees from different companies.

Knowing what allowances were included in a proposal, you can do a little math to normalize the proposals. The difference in the allowances between #! And #2 is ~$3,000, and between #2 and #3 it is ~$3,500. If you add $3,000 plus 50 percent markup to price #1, and subtract $3,500 plus 50 percent markup from price #3, you find out that these three different proposals are nearly identical. But if all you ever saw was the Total Cost, you would **never** think these proposals could be equivalent.

This is why you should always insist that allowances be used and declared in every remodeling proposal you accept.
When you normalize prices this way in the real world, they will seldom be identical. But after adjusting for different allowances, you can still learn a lot! The price difference after adjusting is almost exclusively due to the different markup (overhead plus profit) for each company.

All businesses cover costs like rent, phones, utilities, vehicles, advertising, insurance, employee benefits, administrative salaries, and other non-project-related costs by charging overhead. Overhead is added on top of all labor, material, and subcontractor costs.

Typically, small companies have small overhead expenses and large ones have larger overhead expenses.

This is because every item or service that is included in a remodeling proposal (or contract) also includes a markup. That markup is comprised of the remodeler's overhead expenses plus their profit margin. A company with larger overhead will always cost more for the very same project than a low-overhead company because their non-job-related expenses are larger. They may have a showroom, a fleet of trucks, managers who are office-only employees, or bigger advertising budgets. Those overhead costs exist for all companies to a degree, but the largest ones have far larger overhead expenses and they pass on those costs to you.

Adjusting for allowances lets you see the markup differences of the bidders in terms of total dollars. It's a nice piece of information to have. But honestly, based on my explanation above and your observations of each remodeler's advertising, website, vehicles, specialty employees, office/showrooms, etc., you probably could surmise this already. Calculating their different core amounts (without allowances included) simply confirms it.

Allowance Saving Technique

A significant additional pricing benefit can be gained when using allowances if you simply declare to the bidders, "I want you to use the following allowances in preparing your proposals" (and then give them a list of allowance figures to use when estimating). When all your bidders use the exact same allowance figures for those items and services, it equalizes the single biggest price variable between proposals (eliminating too-high and too-low allowances). It also stabilizes their markups. Since a markup is charged on every dollar included in an estimate, reducing the values used in the estimate also reduces markup costs by the same percentage. This practice will limit the typically large difference in total markup as you saw in the prior example.

Taking this to the extreme, if you told everyone to allow just $1,000 for new cabinets and $1,000 for new countertops (figures that are absurdly low), what have you done? You have reduced the allowance figures of a typical kitchen by perhaps ten to fifteen thousand dollars, and also reduced the amount of total markup included. This reduces your contractor-based costs to a much lower total figure. **Be aware that when you do this, YOU are still responsible for paying the additional costs between the allowed amounts and the real-life price of cabinets and tops (or whatever allowance category the allowance covers).** But if you are self-funding your project, this works very much in your favor. With some bank loans, this would not be possible. It only works when the homeowner has control over disbursement of funds.

Buy Your Own Appliances

If you are comfortable going to Menards, Home Depot, Lowes, or other local appliance shops and signing an agreement to purchase your own appliances for the kitchen remodel, do it. This way you pay the actual cost of the appliance without remodeler markups.

The discount cost to the remodeler for buying most appliances is so small as to be nonexistent. And their markups are from 20 percent to 60 percent, so it is to your advantage to remove those product costs from the price and save. Besides, the local appliance dealers usually work directly with homeowners, and often will provide free delivery. So you can almost totally eliminate markup and profit on all appliances in your project.

In modest kitchens, this may save $1,000, while in upscale kitchens, you could save up to $15,000 or more. Why pay your remodeler to turn around and charge you extra for the same items that the vendor is happy to sell you directly?

If you use a kitchen and bath specialty remodeler, you may already be obligated to use their brands of appliances or their vendors. Be sure to check that out in advance before signing. They may not allow you to buy your own appliances.

Supply It Yourself

There are a number of products that you should simply supply yourself. These items include most of the taste-driven choices for your kitchen, which can play a significant part in the final look you are trying to achieve.

In most of these cases I suggest that you inform your remodeler prospects that you intend to purchase and supply the following items for them to install:

- Cabinet knobs/pulls/handles
- Ceiling-mounted light fixtures (**not** recessed, in-ceiling items)
- Ceiling fans
- Wall-mounted lights (vanity, sconces, or exit door lights)

This is not done specifically to save money, though it does save the markup on the products. You do it primarily because it gives you complete control of the final look of the kitchen. All these choices are taste driven, and your impression is the most important one. Besides, architects and remodelers are never right. If they allow $200 for a fixture you would spend $110 on, you think they are driving up the price. If they only allow $50 for an item that you would spend $150 for, you think they are low-balling you. And if they buy a light fixture for you, there's no doubt it would not be the same style you would have selected!

In short, though these expenses are often a small figure, perhaps in the hundreds of dollars, they make a large impact on the final look of the project. So buy these items yourself, supply them or have them delivered to the house, and then have them installed by your remodeler.

Do It Yourself

If there are portions of the work that you really want to do yourself, and for which you have the skill set and experience, then you can inform your prospective bidders that you intend to perform these services.

In my experience, the only service that owners have performed successfully was painting. This does *not* require years of training to do, and it can save hundreds to thousands of dollars based on the size of your project. If you buy all the paint and supplies required, along with some pizza and drinks, you (perhaps with a group of friends) can paint your entire project in an evening or a weekend. Whether you rent the finest equipment available (talk to the nearest professional paint/paint supply store) or do it by hand with brushes and rollers, there are great savings to be had.

Pro Tip:

Paint before the finished floor is in place whenever possible. You don't want to risk spills or drips on your new hardwood, tile, or carpet if they can be avoided.

Also, you should paint kitchens before the cabinets are installed. You can get a prime coat and one or two finish coats in quickly and easily without having to worry about those thousands of dollars of cabinets you might scratch or drip on. After the cabinets and tops are installed, all you have is a few touch-ups that can often be done (carefully) with a brush and a steady hand.

One thing people always ask if they can do to save money is demolition. Why? I think it's because busting walls, cabinets, and floors with a sledgehammer is fun. At least it looks that way on TV, right?

However, the real cost of demolition is not in the busting of walls and tearing down cabinets. It's in the back-breaking work of hauling the bits and debris out of the house and getting them to the dump. If you're not prepared to clean up and dispose of all the debris, then doing the demolition is not a way to save costs or time. And most importantly, when you're taking apart walls, ceilings, etc., you probably don't have the skills to deal with the plumbing and electrical services there, so don't touch those. Please leave that for the pros. Besides, the company you hire does this for a living. They'll do it faster, better, and cheaper than you can.

Finally, it's not in your best interest to do part of the actual construction work yourself. Many contractors don't want the customer (or their friend, family member, or coworker) providing integral services in the middle of the contract. It's a recipe for disaster. If you "know a guy" and want to get "a deal" on a particular phase of your project, my advice is this: don't do it.

But if you insist, then alert every remodeler you interview about your intention to do such-and-such a phase yourself or to have so-and-so do that phase. At least your early disclosure prior to their estimating and proposal writing allows them to adjust the schedule and cover the contingencies. It's always better to ask permission in this case. Never spring a surprise like this on your remodeler after the contract is signed, or you could be in for a very difficult time.

Direct-Pay Option

This option is only applicable when you are self-fund the project (you, not a bank, are making all payments). It also requires the cooperation of your remodeling contractor. It *must* be brought to their attention early in the interview process in the event that they choose not to participate. That could mean finding another firm to interview if one or more are hesitant to allow this option.

I first used the direct-pay option with clients during the economic downturn in 2008, in an effort to be much more cost-competitive and to stay busy. Customers loved it for reasons you'll understand in a moment. I kept signing customers, and they got a top-quality company at a much more affordable price.

This option is the single biggest cost savings advice I know, and it is without any risk. In fact, this tip will not alter the quality or look of your project one iota, but could save you $5,000, $10,000, or even $15,000 on an upscale kitchen remodel.

The direct-pay option works like this: you ask your remodeler to obtain prices, quotes, and bids from their regular vendors and subcontractors for some of the following big-ticket items:

- Hardwood or tile materials
- Cabinets
- Countertops
- Plumbing fixtures
- New exterior doors
- New exterior windows
- Electrician (materials and labor)
- HVAC (materials and labor)

You let the remodelers know that you wish to pay selected vendors or subcontractors directly (instead of you paying the remodeler and them paying the vendor). The remodeler presents you with the vendor's price quote, invoice, or bid, and you use your checkbook or credit card to immediately pay the invoice price.

Because you agree to work with their regular vendors and subcontractors, your contractor knows that they get to maintain control over the orders, schedule, and quality. However, when using this option, you should also suggest to your remodelers (or expect them to suggest to you) that they maintain a 10 percent markup on the list of direct-pay expenses as a management fee to offset their time obtaining pricing and doing the ordering of the DP items on your behalf.

How does this benefit you? The largest benefit is a significant cost savings. With the total cost of the list of direct-pay items and services out of your contract, your savings are approximately equal to the overhead percentage of the remodeler. Smaller remodelers with lower overhead (20 to 25 percent) result in slightly less savings to you, while larger remodelers (overheads from 40 to 60 percent) would result in much larger savings. So doing this with upscale and large projects through design-build and large traditional remodelers could result in very large savings. How large? The combined cost of just semi-custom cabinets and stone tops in a nice kitchen could easily exceed $20,000. This means your savings could be $6,000 at a 30 percent markup or $10,000 at a 50 percent markup. The cost of installed hardwood floors, the plumber, and the electrician could also reach $20,000—meaning additional direct-pay savings for you.

If the direct-pay option is something you desire to use for your project, then you should only obtain proposals from remodelers who are willing to cooperate with you. The only way to find out who will agree to do the direct-pay option is to ask them. So be certain to bring it up during your initial interviews. I think it's an important item to place in the introduction of your Project Packet as well so they cannot misunderstand your intention.

While the direct-pay option sounds very one-sided in favor of the homeowner (it really does offer very large price breaks to those who use it), there are some benefits to the remodeler too. First, the involved subs and suppliers get paid immediately by you. Typically, they invoice the contractor about thirty days after service and get paid another thirty days after that. And let's face it, the remodeler has a few less bills and payments to worry about!

Second, remodelers who employ this option often make more sales by remaining more price competitive. They also lower their income taxes and their insurance fees slightly (both of which are based on the total dollars of revenue through the company).

Don't get me wrong, the homeowner benefit is huge by comparison. But if it means making the sale and getting a project or losing the sale to a company that will cooperate, many remodelers will agree to work with this option. Just be sure they know about it up front. **Never** spring this on a contractor as a last-minute suggestion.

Pro Tip:

For projects where you control the payments (not the bank), use the *Direct-Pay Option (DP)* with your remodeler. The contractor allows you to pay for select big-ticket items, subs, and materials directly to their regular vendors. You receive reduced or eliminated overhead (markup) on the DP products and services, a substantial savings.

For the contractor, this is better than you insisting on buying and supplying the parts and pieces on your own. The Direct-Pay Option allows the contractor to maintain control of the orders, performance, schedules, etc. And they are always more comfortable working with suppliers and subs they use regularly. Your major benefits are substantial savings and getting their trade pricing.

So let the pros arrange the deals, and you simply pay directly and save.

"Double Dip" Savings with Direct-Pay

There is a second significant benefit of using the direct-pay option. As mentioned earlier (when I told you about signature loans), using your credit cards to pay for remodeling expenses has its privileges. You not only enjoy the direct-pay overhead savings outlined above, but you reap the benefits of the card you use to make those payments (cash back, airline miles, or points). You actually save on the initial contract, then again whenever you make your direct-pay payments using your card! Just be certain that you pay off the entire balance of that card monthly to avoid the high interest charges.

Pro Tip:

Remember to use your credit card whenever possible on these purchases to get a **second** benefit: card rewards (cash back, points, or miles).

"Savings" Options to Avoid!

I've shown you several great ways to save money without affecting the quality of the end product. Don't gamble on cheap products or vendors. Don't compromise on the quality of your results. You get what you pay for.

For myriad reasons, I recommend that you don't buy and supply other products and materials for your job. This because you simply don't have the same number and quality of contacts and sources that your remodeler has. You don't work with the vendors regularly so that you can get immediate help and cooperation when needed. You also don't get trade pricing like your contractors receive.

I suggest using your remodeler's regular suppliers, vendors, and subs whenever possible. Take all the help and guidance their trade partners have to offer. Not to mention the cost discounts.

Next, always, ignore price clubs, outlets, and bargain stores. Their quality **never** compares with the lines and products at your remodeler's regular vendors. Your contractor also gets a significant trade discount from the vendor that the public cannot get, so it's often the lowest cost, best-quality cabinet option.

When something happens mid-project, you want your contractor to make the calls and solve the problem. God forbid if your cabinet order was wrong, or a critical part was missing and work had to stop three to four weeks while you tracked down the replacement parts.

Additionally, **DO NOT** order appliances or plumbing fixtures from the internet! While it may appear that you could save a few dollars over the same items sold in your town or by the vendors your remodeler uses, your savings will be erased (and then some) if you ever need to make a warranty claim. Use **ONLY** local merchants to purchase appliances and plumbing fixtures so that service calls and repairs are easily performed by local agents on items they sell and service regularly

Finally, the very last thing you ever want to do is try and save money by hiring a cheap remodeler. You **do not** save money when you seek the low-price contractor. As the Chinese Proverb goes: "When you pay peanuts, you get monkeys".

"If you think it's expensive hiring a professional, wait until you hire an amateur."

Red Adair

Section 5:
THROUGH MY EYES

As an architect and remodeler, I know which Feature and Function decisions must be made first, which cost more (or less), and which choices typically make-or-break a kitchen design.

Now let's take an in-depth look, through my eyes, at the critical decisions and choices faced in a typical kitchen remodel. It's the same information I look for when I interview clients planning kitchen remodels.

You've already generated a draft Project Packet that includes your Need List, Wish List, Budget, and your Selection Table. This section allows you to update some of your decisions based on this unique look at kitchen design fundamentals.

Updating your Project Packet this way allows your kitchen designer and remodeler to provide a spot-on custom solution for your new kitchen.

Chapter 30

Step 1 – Major Decisions

Most kitchen material selection deadlines follow the construction order which means they need to be chosen and ordered sooner if they are to be installed sooner. So kitchen shopping (and decision making) does not actually begin with the items people typically look at first—countertops, tile backsplashes, and paint colors. These cosmetic materials and choices are among the last needed, and are also among the easiest to order and install.

Some items have long lead-times, which means they take an unusually long time from ordering to delivery. That means such items need to be selected and ordered a bit earlier in the process. Cabinets are one example of this, taking between one and four months to be delivered after an order is placed. The higher-end the cabinet chosen, the longer the lead-time. So naturally, cabinet selection becomes one of the early items to make decisions about.

Long before the permit is issued and construction begins, these critical choices and decisions are needed by the architect or kitchen designer who will lay out your new kitchen.

I've made the following nine-point checklist of important choices you will need to make before a realistic solution can be designed for your kitchen:

1. Method(s) of cooking.
2. List of major appliances.
3. Types of in-kitchen eating.
4. Island or peninsula.
5. Basic cabinet information.
6. Type and number of sinks.
7. Countertop material preference.
8. Floor material preference.
9. Focal point.

Let's take a look at each major decision on the checklist separately, so you understand what you need to decide in advance, and why it's important.

1. Method of Cooking

The designer needs an understanding of how you will cook and eat in the new kitchen, as well as how many people will use it, and the key features to be used in the design.

In decision #1, Method of Cooking, you simply decide if you will use a stove or range, or if you will use a cooktop with separate ovens instead. Then, consider how many ovens you need.

These basic answers are usually pretty easy for most of us. If you're stuck on range vs. cooktop, then you know what you need to consider and decide first! It's not that you need to know the exact brand, size, etc. But one type of cooking is self-contained in 30 to 48 inches (stove/range), and the other usually takes up twice as much space split between two locations (cooktop plus ovens). Without knowing this preference, your architect or kitchen designer would need to design two kitchens in order to get one idea that might be reasonable. So help them out and make this your first major decision.

After you know how you want to cook, you can take more time to figure the out brand, model, size and other features a bit later on. But get each of the nine major decisions made before you get wrapped up in the final choices and selections of your materials.

2. Major Appliances

In decision #2, you make a list of the Major Appliances you want in your new kitchen. You already chose a range or a cooktop with separate ovens—which is answer a or b below. Now it's time for a touch more info on those cooking choices, as well as some other appliance information.

By determining the size and quantity of appliances, you help your designer allot enough space in the design.

These answers also inform your designer about which services (gas, electric, plumbing) are required, so they can make smart decisions in those regards.

Your appliance selections will include many of the following:
    a)   Oven/range info: Size/burners? Gas or electric?
Or...
    b)   Cooktop: Number of burners? Fuel?
Wall ovens: How many? What width? Gas or electric?
    c)   Refrigerator: Type/style? Size?
    d)   Freezer: With refrigerator or separate?
    e)   Microwave: Type? Location (counter, under cabinet, over range, drawer)
    f)   Dishwasher (standard, 2 or drawers?)
    g)   Other: Trash compactor? Ice maker? Wine fridge?

Even though you already selected a or b, you can now determine if the fuel will be electric or gas (including LP) and how many burners the cooking surface will have. The number of burners goes hand-in-hand with the size of the range or cooktop to determine the width (size) of most cooking appliances. Even if you **may** change the number of burners or the size of the appliance in the future, aim for the larger of the options.

Once again this is so the architect or kitchen designer can get everything into the design and make it work. It's easier to take up six inches later with a slightly bigger cabinet, than it is to steal six inches to fit in a larger cooking surface when the rest of the kitchen is already planned.

If you are planning a cooktop, you then need to decide if the ovens will be stacked and built into a wall cabinet, or if they will both be under-counter ovens. In most kitchens, one of those two ovens will be the microwave, or perhaps a dual-purpose microwave/convection oven.

And just because you use a range (oven and cooking surface combined in one appliance), that does not prohibit you from having additional ovens. Make a note of how many you need, regardless of your cooking choice.

Most of us select a refrigerator (c) and freezer (d) combined into a single appliance. The traditional width of that unit today is 36 inches wide. Do not allow less space than this in your kitchen. Even if you use something smaller now, one day that fridge will fail and it will be replaced by a full-sized fridge. Build the larger space into the plan for ease of everyone down the line.

Traditional refrigerators stick out forward of the cabinet faces by eight or nine inches. If this is troubling to you, or the designer does not have that amount of space, you can select a counter-depth fridge. However, counter-depth fridges need more width than a standard fridge to give you the same cubic feet of storage. Your designer needs to know if you want a standard fridge or a counter-depth unit and the width you prefer so they can reserve enough space in the plan for the unit.

The same is true in upscale kitchens when you might use a full-sized refrigerator only along with a full-size separate freezer. Once again, your designer needs to save enough space for both, so tip them off about the units' size that you prefer (even if you have not selected the final units yet).

It's very likely that you'll have a microwave (e) oven in your new kitchen. If it is over your 30-inch range then you know it's width. If it is built-in along with a wall oven in a wall oven cabinet, then it is likely to be a smaller unit, sized similarly to the other oven. In the event you want it placed below a countertop, perhaps in an island, then it will be yet another dimension.

Because all microwaves are different sizes with different controls, it behooves you to make this selection in advance so the designer is working with your first choice as they design the new layout.

When it comes to dishwashers (f), 95 percent of them are 24 inches wide and counter depth. If this will be your case, great, just pass that on and make your final selection later.

In the event you want drawer dishwashers, that should be worked out in advance so they can be sized and placed on the first design draft. There are fewer manufacturers and sizes of drawer units, so it would be smart to make your choice in advance. They are considerably more costly than the best full-size dishwashers, and the plumbing install costs are also higher, but they are a wonderful luxury if the cost does not scare you away.

There are a number of other minor appliances that may tickle your fancy for the new kitchen. If you are interested in other appliances (g) like a trash compactor, ice maker, or wine fridge, please make your decisions in advance and inform your designer what size unit(s) you prefer, so they can work it into your kitchen design from the start. Like with other appliances, it's better to include this if you're serious, and choose the slightly larger one for your first design. Once again—it's easier to fill that space with cabinets later than it is to make room for an appliance that was not designed in to begin with.

3. In-Kitchen Eating

Most kitchens have eating as their next function after storage and preparation of food. So it's presumed that you will eat in your new kitchen. If this is not true, please make that very clear in your Project Packet and your discussions with the kitchen designer.

For those who will include eating in their new kitchen layout, you need to determine which way (or ways) you will eat there.

The traditional solution is a table and chairs. If this is your choice, you must determine the table shape (square, round, or rectangle) and the maximum number of chairs you need. Tables are huge space hogs in a kitchen, requiring room for the table, each chair (occupied), and room to walk past the table on multiple sides.

My strong suggestion if you have a smaller kitchen with an adjacent dining room is to eliminate the kitchen table. Build yourself more kitchen instead of squeezing a second table in there, less than 15 or 20 feet from the one in the next room (not to mention the one on the deck or patio 20 feet in the other direction).

Tables require lots of space, so the kitchen needs to have lots of space for the table and chairs. If yours does have the room, work out the table you need, so your designer has the best information they need.

The alternate kitchen seating options include seating at islands and peninsulas, also known as *counter seating*. This is smarter in most kitchens because the seating is adjacent to expanded storage and work areas, and not a space hog that denies the kitchen the storage and work room it requires.

The drawbacks of counter seating are that it is not moveable, it's not easy to seat more than four people in many kitchens, and you can't typically sit "around" the counter for easy conversation. I'm nitpicking here since these are not horrible problems, and top designers can make counter seating look and work great.

Counter seating does not literally need to be at counter height (36 inches) either. It can be lower (at table height of 29-30 inches), or higher (at bar height of 42 inches). In the case of the lower option, traditional eating chairs or stools can be used. In the taller cases, there are hundreds of styles of stools for counters at those heights.

So, consider the minimum seating you need in your kitchen, and decide if that will occur at a table or an island or peninsula. Then let your architect or kitchen designer know your preference.

4. Islands and Peninsulas

I just mentioned kitchen islands and peninsulas as seating options in kitchens, and they certainly can be that. But it is not necessary for islands or peninsulas to have seating at all. First and foremost, they are ways to get greater amounts of kitchen cabinet storage and countertop workspace.

An island "floats" in the kitchen, unattached to any walls or other cabinetry in the kitchen. Its sides are all exposed, and you can walk around it. Think Hawaii.

By contrast, a peninsula has one of its sides touching a wall or touching other cabinetry, and the rest projecting out into the floorspace of the kitchen. Think Florida.

Both meet the demand for additional base cabinet storage and extra working countertop area. Both could possibly house an appliance, with sinks and cooktops being most common. Both could also have some eating seating as an integral part of them. Both require extra care from your designer to make sure they do not restrict the circulation in the kitchen and choke the workspace allotted.

Like tables, islands and peninsulas are space hogs, taking up lots of very valuable floorspace in a kitchen. But since they combine storage, additional countertop workspace, and occasionally counter seating, they offer a lot more to a kitchen than a free-standing table possibly can.

The key with islands and peninsulas is making them fit comfortably in the kitchen without compromising the working areas and circulation through the room. I discuss this in the next chapter and explain how you should look at your new kitchen spatially as you begin planning.

But when they fit properly, islands and peninsulas can offer your kitchen a good-looking option with lots of extra storage, workspace, and seating. You decide now; then work with your designer on their size and whether or not they fit properly.

5. Basic Cabinet Information

Most base cabinets are 24 inches deep from the wall to the door and drawer surface. And most wall cabinets are 12 inches deep from the wall to the door surface. And most cabinets come in 3-inch width increments from about 9 inches wide up to about 48 inches wide.

Despite those commonalities, when you look around, you see how different one kitchen is from another, despite being constructed from the same, basic pieces.

In the end, the cabinet you select will play a large role in the look of your finished kitchen, as well as its storage capacity and ease of use. It's an important choice in each and every kitchen.

But shopping for kitchens is a lot like shopping for used cars if you do it wrong (like most folks). So I always tried to simplify the process for my clients, and will try to help you simplify your cabinetry choices also.

Please understand there are over 400 lines of cabinets in the US alone, and nearly all of them offer the same looks as all the other brands. So the least important thing to fixate on when starting a kitchen design is, "Whose cabinets will I use?"

The best thing to decide when first thinking about a new kitchen and preparing your Project Packet is, "How do I want my new cabinets to look?", and "What special features do I need included?". With those two answers your kitchen designer has the information needed to start planning the new kitchen, and your remodeler can prepare a solid ballpark estimate of the cabinet cost. At this point in the process, that's exactly what you need. You'll make your final choices of brand, line, features, etc. later on after selecting your remodeler and signing a contract. No need to waste a single moment of worry on that idea at this time.

Regardless of where you look at cabinets (cabinet showrooms, big box stores, online), you really have just four simple cabinet factors to decide on before your designer can move ahead with confidence.

- Cabinet door **material** (face & doors of solid wood, or other materials)
- Cabinet **finish** (painted or stained wood surfaces, or laminate surface)
- Door **style** (slab door, raised panel door, or flat panel door)
- Door **type** (standard overlay, full overlay, flush/inset)

Dozens of cabinet brands make each wood cabinet style you might select. Numerous brands make the high-pressure laminate cabinet looks you might choose. Again, you are not shopping brand right now; you are capturing the look you want, and brand selection will come later.

Cabinet Material

The doors, drawers, and face frames of most cabinets will either be made of a solid wood (like oak, maple, hickory, cherry, etc.) or they will be an inexpensive wood product covered with high-pressure laminate.

Clearly, laminate cabinets will not be confused with wood cabinets.

If you prefer a high-tech look with clean lines, unique color looks, or super smooth surfaces, then plan to use laminated cabinets.

If you like any of the dozens of traditional kitchen styles (regardless of the look of the doors), then you should select from available wood cabinets.

It should take no more than fifteen to twenty minutes in a cabinet shop to look at sample doors and decide if you like the sleek, modern look of laminates, or if you prefer the more traditional looks provided by wood.

Cabinet Finish

Once you know whether you will use laminate or wood finished cabinets, the next choice is the "finish" you prefer for those cabinets.

Laminate cabinets are pretty easy… they're laminate. Choose them and you can consider the color you prefer or just move ahead to your next decision.

If you are using wood cabinets, then your finish choices begin with selecting painted cabinets or stained cabinets. This distinction is easy to understand and they look totally different. Fifteen minutes will be enough to determine if you prefer paint or stain.

In many cases it boils down to this: do you want to see the wood grain, or do you prefer a solid color cabinet? If you like the wood to show, then stain is the best option. Most solid colors are paint finishes.

Please note that you can get a wide range of "colors" regardless of the wood species you select. Final color on wood cabinets is largely determined by the stain and not just the wood itself. Most manufacturers offer from four to ten different color choices in each wood species they offer. So achieving a cherry look can happen with cherry, birch, or maple woods. This gives you a wide price range in the event that your budget isn't unlimited!

Don't sweat the exact laminate choice or the precise stain or paint to use on your cabinets. That will be a color choice that also works with your flooring, your countertop, the room paint color, and perhaps your tile backsplash. Yes, it's easier to start with the flooring and cabinets and work your way up the room, but you don't need to know the exact color of the finish, just the type to get your designer off and running.

Door Style

The third of four cabinet factors you need to choose for your kitchen designer is the door style. This choice has a big impact on the final look of the kitchen and on the cabinet cost. By thinking about this option now instead of later, the initial cabinet cost estimates are more accurate, and based on your exact preference.

Cabinet doors come in three basic styles: slab doors, flat-panel doors, and raised-panel doors.

Cabinet Door <u>STYLES</u>

SLAB DOOR   FLAT PANEL   RAISED PANEL

Slab doors are exactly what the name implies–one big slab of wood. These doors are actually many pieces of your chosen wood put together and made into a large, flat slab. The edges might be rounded or squared, but a smooth slab of wood (with the finish of your choice) is what you get.

Slab doors lean toward a more modern, sleek look from a wood door. Based on your paint or stain choice and your hardware selection, the kitchen could go from rustic to high-tech with this door choice.

Two factors of note with the slab door: they cost more than flat- and raised-panel doors, and the largest ones are prone to warp. When these are wider than 21 inches, or extremely tall (like on pantry cabinets), they are prone to warping over time.

Flat-panel doors also are exactly what the name implies. The panel in the middle of the door frame is flat, not raised. Sometimes the flat panel is solid wood, and sometimes it is veneer, but it is always flat. These are the simplest doors to make, and they are often the least costly door choice.

The most common flat-panel door around is the Shaker style door which has many variations.

These doors are simple looking and can be gorgeous with stain or paint finishes. It typically uses concealed hinges on its doors.

The raised-panel door is a frame with a center panel, but this panel is not flat, it is raised. The panel projects forward toward the viewer in the third dimension. In many ways this is a very traditional cabinet. The wall cabinets can have a square, arched, or cathedral top to the raised panel, while the lower base cabinets are always square topped. Drawers can be five-piece drawers if large enough, or they can be slab fronts.

Paint or stain finishes are possible with these doors, though they are most commonly stained to keep with the more traditional look they offer.

Because flat-panel and the raised-panel doors have multi-piece frames of solid wood, they are not prone to the same warpage issues as the slab doors. They both use less wood than the slab door, so they are typically less costly as well.

When you choose which style of door you prefer, put that into your Project Packet so your designer knows and the estimate will reflect it.

Door Type

Cabinet doors come in three basic types. These types refer to how the door looks while it fills or covers the hole on the face frame of the cabinet. The three styles are flush or inset doors, standard or traditional overlay doors, and full overlay doors.

Cabinet Door TYPES

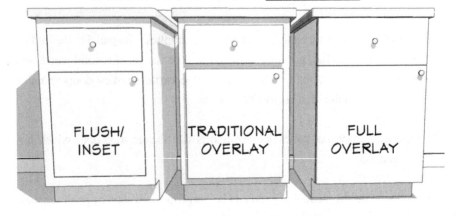

FLUSH/ INSET   TRADITIONAL OVERLAY   FULL OVERLAY

As with the door styles, the names give you an understanding of how each door type works. The flush/inset door literally fills the hole in the frame, and when closed, the door or drawer face is flush with, or set inside the face frame of the cabinet.

This was a very popular furniture style during the 1900's in the US. It was also used by skilled craftsmen on handmade kitchen cabinets as opposed to average craftsmen who would choose the easier overlay style door.

When you take a look at a flush/inset door or drawer you'll probably decide instantly if the look is for you or not. If you're looking for a high-tech or modern look, the answer is automatically no.

It's also important to note two drawbacks of this type door and drawer face. First, this style is harder to make and requires more human involvement at the factory. Therefore, it's the most-costly type of door and drawer face. Second, because these must precisely fit inside the frame of the cabinet, any small change in alignment is easily seen. The tolerance for fitting or adjusting this type of door and drawer front is small and unforgiving. For these reasons, you often see beaded edges on the face frame to hide minor misalignments.

The overlay door types (traditional overlay and full overlay) both *overlay* the opening in the face frame. This means the doors and drawer fronts are larger than the hole they cover, and the doors themselves ride on the outside surface of the face frame.

The traditional overly door and drawer front simply covers the hole by a small margin, leaving most of the cabinet face frame exposed to the room on all four sides of the door and drawer. This is the most common type of cabinet door in most homes for the latter half of the 1900's. Almost all of us have lived in homes with kitchen and bathroom cabinets that had this type of door and drawer fronts.

The overlay hides any intolerance between the drawer or door and the hole in the frame. This style of door can use traditional knuckle hinges that are exposed to the room, or concealed hinges.

The full overlay door and drawer type is once again explained well by its name. The doors and drawers still overlay the holes in the cabinet face frame, but this time they *fully* overlay the frame, almost completely hiding it.

This door type gives the same impression as a square-edged slab door, or most laminate doors, and it works well for sleek, modern, high-tech looks in kitchens and baths.

What's interesting in the past thirty years is the proliferation of the flat panel door style in the full overlay door type. The most common examples are the Shaker and modified Shaker doors in wide use these days. These offer an upscale, modern look from an old-time style. They also work well in both paint and in stain finishes.

With this basic grasp of the door types, choose the one you want to start with and make sure your Project Packet reflects that for the benefit of your kitchen designer.

6. Sinks

Most kitchens only need one sink. A second sink is usually unnecessary. They are definitely costly, and they take up a lot of valuable floor space by creating another workstation. Every family should make their own decision if a second sink is a need or a luxury. Add them only in kitchens with plenty of extra room and a good-sized budget.

For each sink in your planned kitchen, your designer wants to know what sink type and what sink size you would like.

Sink size is simple, the width of the sink is the critical number since it determines the minimum size cabinet the sink will fit into. With almost no exceptions, sinks fit into a standard depth countertop and cabinet that is nominally 24 inches deep.

The width of sinks is based first on the number of sink basins (1, 2, or 3). The size of the basins is an important factor in all sinks since it determines what will fit in your sink. Regardless of the number of basins you select, be sure they are all wide enough for your everyday cooking and cleaning tasks.

An oversized single-basin sink versus a double-basin sink is a personal choice. Neither one is dramatically better than the other. Each homeowner's preference is the deciding factor. My experience is evenly split between oversized single- and double-basin sinks, with about 1 percent going for triple basin sinks.

The second sink factor is the type of sink. This refers to how the sink fits into/onto the cabinet and countertop. The two most common sink mounting types are overlay sinks and undermount sinks.

Their names describe how they mount with relation to the countertop, one overlaying the counter surface (often with a bead of caulk sealing it down to the countertop), and the other mounting to the underside of the countertop from below.

The most common overlay sink materials are stainless steel and china sinks used on laminate countertops. This mount is essentially required since the laminate only protects the top surface of the wooden countertop material, and the core of the countertop cannot be exposed to water.

Undermount sinks expose the top and core of the countertop material to your view and to water, so they are exclusively used on man-made solid surface tops and on real stone countertops.

One advantage of the undermount sink type is that water and crumbs on the counter surface are easily brushed into the sink without getting caught on the sink edge (as they typically do with overlay sinks).

Another advantage of undermount sinks is that they are automatically deeper than overlay sinks since the thickness of the top is added to the depth of the sink. This can add 1 to 1 ½ inches of depth in the sink without buying a deeper sink.

The other common sink type is a farmhouse or apron sink. These sinks are a large-format sink that can be china, stainless steel, or enamel on steel, and they typically have a finished front of that same material that protrudes forward of the cabinet face. They require a special sink cabinet, so if you intend to use a farmhouse or apron sink, it is essential to let the designer and remodeler know.

Once you have selected your preferred sink size (width based on single or double basins) and you know the type (overlay or undermount), include that information in your Project Packet so it gets to your designer as they get started. You can make the final choice of brand, material, etc. later on, but these factors are the ones required before design begins.

7. Countertop Preference

There are many different materials used as kitchen countertops these days. But many of those materials are not common (such as stainless steel, zinc, paper, bamboo, etc.). The most common countertop materials are laminate, man-made solid-surface, wood, and stone tops. I'll do a super-quick pro/con review of each so you have an overview of these materials.

Laminate tops have been in use since the 1950's. They encapsulate a solid color, a patterned print, or a photo image inside a multi-layered plastic layer that gets glued to a wooden countertop form. Since the proliferation of laminate flooring, people have embraced the improved technology, and laminate countertops have also changed for the better since Grandma's kitchen.

PROS: They are the least expensive top of the four main materials. They require no maintenance other than cleaning.

CONS: You need to pay more for invisible seams and edges. They scratch and burn easily and there's no simple way to repair those defects. They are not ideal for undermount sinks. They can break down above dishwashers (since the humidity and heat can cause the wood to swell and glues to dissolve over time).

Solid-surface tops are man-made of resins and plastics. They are a solid material throughout from top to bottom. The brand name most people know is Corian by DuPont, but there are many manufacturers.

PROS: They are the same color throughout. Their seams can be made to blend and disappear during installation. Seamless sinks (made with the same material as the top) are common. Burns and scratches can be buffed and polished out in many cases (by pros or homeowners). They offer solid colors and many stone-look options.

CONS: These tops are still expensive today. The prices have not dropped much to remain cost-effective in the face of much lower-cost granite tops this past decade. They are soft and scratch and burn easily. Though homeowners can buff or polish many minor scratches themselves, this often changes the sheen (unless the repair is performed professionally, which is costly). Their long-term durability is not great. They stain easily from things like meats, OJ, lemon juice, beets, wine, etc.

While they were the first material to offer a seamless look, no-lip sinks, and a massive upgrade from laminates, they are headed for the dinosaur pile unless they find a way to lower their prices dramatically.

Wood tops are actually quite common today. They may not be used in the entire kitchen, but they are no longer just used as a cutting board or for rolling carts. Wood (including bamboo, which is actually a form of grass) is used all over kitchens these days.

Wood tops can be very inexpensive (bamboo and butcher block especially), and they can get costly when custom made from exotic woods by hand.

PROS: Inexpensive to make and install. Can be refinished. Can be replaced. Can have a number of color options from light to dark, plus stripes and checkerboard looks. They get a natural oil finish and are totally safe for foods. They are easy to maintain with occasional oiling to keep them sealed. They are natural materials (green and safe).

CONS: They are wood and they are **not waterproof**. They must be maintained with occasional oiling. They scratch fairly easily. (This varies by the species of wood used and style of top).

Wood tops offer many looks, edges, and colors and a warmth not found in any other top material. They may not be ideal on every surface in the kitchen, but they can be bought and replaced for less than the purchase price of most stone tops. They are ideal for islands and for peninsula eating areas and specific workstations, but perhaps other tops work better around sinks unless you are fastidious and very careful with stray water.

Stone tops are generally divided into the two main stones used in kitchens: granite and quartz. Both stones provide us with countertops that are quite durable, scratch and cut resistant, and heat and stain resistant.

Granite is taken from the ground in giant blocks and sliced like bread to make thin slabs used in our kitchens. Since it's sliced from one larger block, it always has slight color and pattern variation from slab to slab. Everyone uses the same color names for granite, but with the understanding that there is a variety of color and pattern within each name.

Granite is slightly porous, so it can absorb tiny amounts of liquids. This means it needs to be sealed (surface sprayed and wiped down) once or twice a year. If unsealed, granite can get water marks or some stains, or hold bacteria.

Quartz is a crystalline rock that gets crushed and placed into molds with resins and epoxy to form a super-hard, liquid- and stain-proof surface that requires no sealing. Since it is "fabricated," seams between the pieces can disappear, giving the illusion of a single piece of stone. Quartz comes in solid colors and stone-like looks to work with most kitchen color schemes.

PROS: Quartz stone tops offer extreme durability, cut and scratch resistance, liquid resistance, heat resistance, and a wide variety of colors and patterns. Granite is also very attractive and durable, and its colors in the lower price groups are affordable compared to other top materials.

While not the least costly tops, stone tops offer so many colors and durability advantages, they have become the tops of preference in today's kitchen remodeling climate.

CONS: Granite tops require occasional sealing, and can get watermarks or stains if not sealed. Granite (like wood) has patterns and grain, so the edges where pieces join are often visible. Higher-end price groups of granite and all quartz tops are very costly. Fancier edge shapes are a costly upgrade. Some quartz colors are very man-made looking, and sterile or phony in appearance.

As with other selections in this predesign checklist, you do not need to know the exact final choice and all the details. But if you want stone tops with a wood island top, that is what the designer needs to know when laying things out and preparing your estimate. The final edge and finish color can be decided later with no impact on the design, and only a minor one on the cost.

8. Flooring Preference

The last item to preselect in this kitchen predesign checklist is the finished flooring material. The days of linoleum and sheet vinyl floors in our kitchens are over. Laminate, tile, and various woods are the most common flooring materials used in today's kitchens.

As with the other materials we just covered, you do not need to decide the exact details of the flooring you'll use for your kitchen. But choosing between laminate, tile, and wood flooring gives the architect and kitchen designer the right information to plan your new layout and set a realistic flooring allowance in their preliminary price estimate.

Laminates are relatively new on the flooring scene, becoming very popular over the last 15 years. They have similar properties to some of the best countertop laminates, often with a simple-to-install click-together locking system.

PROS: Least expensive flooring material when compared to tile and wood. Easiest and quickest flooring to install. Comes in many looks: solid colors, tile looks, and wood looks. Easy to clean. No significant maintenance required.

CONS: It's plastic, and it has a "tic-tic-tic" sound when walked on in hard soles or by dogs. It can scratch pretty easily. It is smooth and somewhat reflective, so it never truly looks like wood or stone/tile when installed.

Wood flooring has never been more popular in American kitchens than it is today. Better finishes (factory prefinished and better on-site finishes) mean wood floors are more durable and less prone to water damage than ever before. It comes in many different wood species (and in bamboo too), giving many grain and color options. It comes in many widths as well.

Wood offers a rich and warm look to almost any style kitchen. The prefinished material is fast and easy to install. And wood floors can be sanded and refinished several times over the long life of the home to remain a high-quality floor for decades.

PROS: Warm looks, with many colors, species, and grain patterns. Intermediate price point (between laminates and tile). It is durable and can be refinished. It's easy to clean and maintain. It goes with a wide variety of looks from rustic to ornate, and blends beautifully into high-tech looks as well. They are warm floors (compared to other materials), and softer on the feet if you spend much time standing while in the kitchen. They are also quieter (sound-deadening) when compared to the other materials.

CONS: Most wood is finished to allow the grain to be seen, and as a result some pieces are darker and some lighter. This is a natural variation, not a defect, but all wood products have this color variability. If this bothers you, find lighter color woods with fine grain structure to minimize the color difference between boards. Wood floors can scratch and gouge fairly easily. Wider planks are considerably more costly than narrower ones.

If you already have hardwood in adjoining rooms that will run through your kitchen, you are committed to that wood (species and size), and your floor will need to be finished on site. In almost all other cases, you're free to choose pre-finished or finish-in-place woods of any species or size that tickles your fancy and works with your chosen kitchen color palate. When you know you want to use wood, be sure to include that as the flooring line item in your Project Packet and fill in the other details (species, plank width, and color of finish) later on.

Tile floors have been used in kitchens for many years, though they have become less popular over the past couple decades. The most common materials used in tile floors are luxury vinyl tile, ceramic tile, and stone tile.

Luxury vinyl tile (LVT) is a softer and warmer floor than its harder tile cousins. It can be glued down and have grout joints as accents, but is most commonly used in a snap-together system not unlike laminate flooring. It can be found with tile looks, but is more commonly made in plank shape like a wood-floor look. It's soft and can be easily cut and applied over any level subfloor, and typically requires no underlayment.

PROS: It's easy to install and can be applied over any flat substrate without underlayment. It's the least costly tiled floor system that is suitable for most homes. The material is not subject to water damage (though you need to be sure moisture can't get around it). It's easy to keep clean.

CONS: It is not tile and not wood. (If you don't mind a material masquerading as another material, and you find one you like visually, then go for it.) It's soft and can be gouged or scratched pretty easily. It's the least used of these kitchen flooring materials.

Ceramic tile is a well-known material that has been used forever. The upscale tiles, especially large-format ones, are still quite popular in upscale kitchens. They are good looking, easy to clean and care for, and long lasting. They must be installed with mastic or mortar and grout in most cases, and they require an additional substrate (stiffening layer of flat material) beneath them, making tile one of the thicker floors you can use. They come in all sizes and looks (solid colors and stone looks), and in the past decade even wood-look tile has become quite popular.

PROS: Ceramic tile is strong, stiff, and durable. It's easy to clean and holds up well over a long lifetime. It's typically waterproof. It's not easy to scratch most tile. You can have many different looks, including inlay designs, stripes, and borders by using different size and style tiles. You can get stone looks at ceramic tile prices. Tile is the best material if you plan to have in-floor heat in your kitchen.

CONS: Tile floors are hard and cold. Tile floors can crack when heavy objects are dropped on them, and cracked tiles are quite difficult to replace properly. (They can be replaced by professionals, but there is often an obvious tell-tale section of bright tile and grout in an otherwise aging floor.)

Stone tile is the same basic material as ceramic tile, but instead of clay with a finished surface, you have sliced stone (solid) as the tile unit. This is the most upscale material for super-high-end kitchens.

PROS: Stone tile has the same basic installation details and benefits of upscale ceramic tile (clean, good-looking, durable, many upscale looks are possible).

CONS: It has the same overall drawbacks as ceramic tile (hard, cold, expensive, can be cracked).

Stone tile is stunning when the right material is selected. However, the cost is also stunning, often running 50 to 200 percent more than tile costs. Installation of top-quality stone also costs 50 percent more than tile installation.

9. Focal Point

Every room has a focal point. It's a Feature in a room that sticks in your memory after the fact. In kitchens it could be almost anything: a custom appliance, some glass-front wall cabinets, a window seat, a great view, a beam, an island or peninsula, custom lighting... you get to choose.

It's not critical what you choose to be the focal point of your kitchen. What is extremely important is that **you choose the focal point**. Communicate that to your kitchen designer or architect and never leave it to chance.
Take stock of the appliances, sink, cabinets, and other feature areas and decide how you want to highlight your kitchen's focal point.

You might want a custom island with high-end granite with custom lighting as your focus. Or, you might prefer a hand-made tile design above your cooktop or range. Maybe you splurge for some amazing pendant lights over the peninsula.

Or perhaps you choose an amazing stone tile floor with heat throughout the room. All that matters is that you don't leave your focal point to chance.

A focal point does not need to cost you more. But if you don't choose a focal point, your room could lack focus and be "blah" even though it functions well.

So go look at some upscale kitchens and pay attention. What are the focal points of other kitchens that you like? Is there one you would like in your kitchen?

Once you have an idea, update your kitchen's Selection Table so this important information gets to your architect or designer.

Update Your Project Packet

As you make each decision on this nine-point checklist, be sure to add your choices to your kitchen's selection table in your Project Packet.

Remember that you do not need to work out 100 percent of the information about every appliance, your cabinets, tops, flooring, etc. There's time for that as you move ahead.

But by making the decisions laid out above before you hand your Project Packet to any architects or remodelers, you're ahead of the game. Your work up front allows the architect or kitchen designer to begin work on a customized design just for you right from the start. This level of information also allows them to make their allowances more accurate when they make their preliminary price estimates.

If you do start to finalize some of these decisions, just keep updating your kitchen selection table in the Project Packet to track the brand, model, color, size, and other critical information of the final items you want to use.

Don't put added pressure on yourself to get everything 100 percent perfect. Make one decision at a time, and then move on to the next choice. Try to keep to the general order I suggested since these choices are necessary to design the best possible kitchen for you and your family.

Chapter 31

Step 2 – Assess the Space

Before I teach you how kitchens are designed, we need to take stock of the bones of the space we have to work with.

Unless your new kitchen is in an addition, or part of a new home (which are both bigger and very different problems to solve), it's necessary to take a hard look at the room being used for the new kitchen. If you were to strip the room down to the studs and plywood subfloor, what is the starting situation you're left with, and what restrictions does it place on the new solution?

This is how your architect or designer will look at the kitchen, and I want you to be able to understand the limitations facing you also. Two benefits of this exercise are that you will grasp what can and can't be done more easily, and you'll have far greater respect for them when they devise a clever solution that overcomes a limitation placed on you by the existing house.

There are three limiting factors placed on you by whatever room your new kitchen will occupy. They are the doors and doorways, the windows, and the walls. You must respect them and acknowledge the restrictions they place on you.

Let's look at them briefly one at a time.

Doors and Doorways

Doors and doorways define how people (traffic) move through the room. Everything else that gets placed in the room either works with the flow of people through the new layout or hinders that flow. Every successful kitchen flows freely, allowing the kitchen functions to take place without restricting traffic into and out of the room.

In addition to recognizing where the doors and doorways are located, active doors are critical. Each door swing must be considered. Hinged doors require lots of floor area when they swing open and closed. They also dictate the direction of travel into the room and initial light switch locations.

Doorways and doors can be moved, but this is not always an easy or inexpensive task. Exterior doors involve structural framing changes in the wall as well as siding replacement or repair. (Based on the siding type that can be very costly.) Interior doors cannot be moved without affecting the adjacent rooms, so first consider the circulation impact in the adjoining space and whether involving both rooms is worth it to change the door location into your kitchen.

If you have two entrances to the kitchen and one that goes to the outside (deck, patio, yard), you can draw lines that connect those on a plan and see how people would ideally move through the room. We like the simplest, most direct path possible. We like going around as few obstructions as possible. And we like a path that is at least 28 to 30 inches wide so we fit without turning sideways.

This is something that most architects and kitchen designers know and intuitively bring to their kitchen layouts, but it's generally new information to homeowners. It is common sense, but when you're not trained to think this way, it is easily overlooked. Violating these simple rules leaves you with a kitchen that is broken and does not work properly.

Windows

Windows are very important to kitchens. Natural light and views are important in any room where you spend so much time. While windows can be closed, moved, or enlarged, doing these has cost implications. Like with doorways, the starting locations and sizes of windows are givens. If they can be used in place, it yields the least-costly kitchen design possible. When the new kitchen cannot be done around the existing window layout, it's important to devise a design that alters them wisely to avoid excess costs.

When we close or move a window to achieve a truly functional kitchen design, the cost of the change is an essential part of the project. But closing or moving a window that is not critical to the function or success of the kitchen adds lots of expense with little payoff.

Like exterior doors, closing or relocating windows forces a major repair on the exterior of the home to properly conceal the old window location. Depending on the exterior siding material of the window wall, that could be a small nuisance (vinyl siding for instance) or a major, costly headache (brick or stone veneer).

Changes to the existing windows must be deliberately considered, and the kitchen design produced with careful regard for their size and location.

Enlarging a window is not nearly as costly or difficult as closing or moving it, since you are only removing more existing siding and you're not required to patch or repair the opening to make it look original. You're simply making the opening larger in one or two directions, and you can trim or repair the edge of the enlarged opening much more simply than the more extreme cases.

I don't mention exterior doors and windows to tell you not to move them. Just be aware that doing so adds a significant invisible cost to the kitchen, not an easy-to-understand cost like cabinets, tops, flooring, or appliances. Paying to change the siding and trim on one side of your home does not sound like an expense that goes with a kitchen remodel—but it is if you close or move doors and windows on that wall!

Walls

Walls provide the boundaries of most rooms in our homes. Existing walls are one of the first things an architect or kitchen designer looks at when considering the new design. Whether there is enough useful wall space is a critical factor in every kitchen that has ever been designed.

Ovens, refrigerators, most base cabinets, and all wall cabinets are typically located against walls. Without walls, kitchen design is hindered. With walls that are broken up with too many doorways and windows, the same problem occurs – there's not enough continuous space to lay out a proper, working kitchen layout. This is why (along with doors and windows), your starting wall inventory is so important to a new kitchen layout.

Removing walls is something quite common in many kitchen remodels with the trend over the past forty years being to open the interior of our homes in the public spaces–kitchen, family, and dining areas. Removing or opening most walls is possible. It's important to note that structural walls (holding up the second floor or roof above) require very careful handling and analysis by an architect or structural engineer before altering. And many interior walls contain plumbing, electrical, and HVAC ductwork that would need to be relocated (if possible and affordable) in order to open up other walls.

Opening walls into adjacent spaces can make living life in the newly combined rooms a wonderful new experience. But your designer must know of your desire to do it from the moment they learn about your project. Otherwise great effort is spent going in the wrong direction. So if you hope to combine your current kitchen and one or more adjacent rooms into one open space, make sure you get that fact into the project description in the elevator pitch and the room description tables as Functions and Features, so they can make the best plan possible the first time without excess work.

If your kitchen is part of an addition, then it's possible the removed wall will have all new windows and doors in it, leaving your new kitchen canvas blank. That new outside wall can then become anything you and your architect can imagine.

Summary

The information gained by considering existing doors, windows, and walls lets any kitchen designer know what can and cannot be done in the space before even considering your kitchen needs and wants.

By taking a long look at your current kitchen and reviewing the existing openings and walls, you will now be able to assess the amount of useful wall space available as you move toward your new kitchen.

Chapter 32

Step 3 – Space Hogs

Many of the kitchen details most homeowners are interested in are very easy to deliver, like roll-out cabinet trays or a tile backsplash.

This is not at all the case with the items I call "space hogs". Space Hogs include:

- Tables with chairs or Islands with stools.
- Regular (non-eating) islands.
- Peninsulas.
- Pantries.
- Refrigerators and freezers.
- Commercial ranges.
- Walkways and circulation.

I have devoted this chapter to Space Hogs to help you understand how important it is to provide yours with enough working room so they fit and function well. These items are often difficult to combine in a kitchen due to their large, bulky nature and the fact that they require so much space to be used properly.

They take up lots of space, and they all require *additional space* to pass by them or to function properly. So it's critical to know which ones are in or out of each new kitchen right from the start.

Here's a rundown of the main space hogs and what you need to know and consider about each.

Tables with Chairs and Eating Islands

Tables and islands were mentioned when we discussed eating in your kitchen. Nothing in a kitchen requires as much square footage as a table and chairs, or an island with seating. So if you will have an eating table or an eating island in your kitchen, it should be the very first thing placed during kitchen design. Otherwise it will get shoehorned into the remaining space after the kitchen is laid out, like in most builder homes.

A significant number of kitchen remodels are performed just because the eating area in a kitchen is too cramped and does not work for the family.

Most pre-1990 kitchens are simply too small for a table or eating island in combination with adequate space to move around. You simply cannot fit an eating island or table with chairs into a kitchen with a 10- to 12-foot dimension in the narrow direction.

In addition to the size of the actual table or island, you need to designate about 24 inches of space for all chairs or stools (during use). You then require a 24-inch minimum buffer of circulation space to pass by seated people.

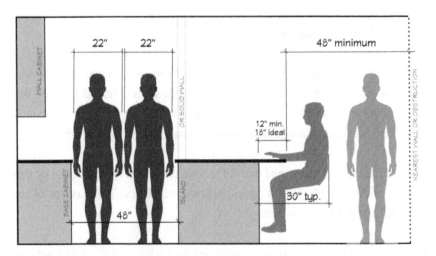

The math tells you there should be 48 inches from any wall to the edge of the table or island, and 48 inches of clear space from the table or island to any other obstructions.

Pro Tip:

Kitchens less than 12 feet wide are almost impossibly small for a table or island without cramping either the seated users or the passersby.

I strongly urge you not to compromise on these minimum clearance dimensions. I never space islands or tables less than 45 inches from the nearest obstruction, and you should not either. Otherwise your new kitchen will be too cramped to use properly when people are seated and eating.

Non-eating Islands

When there is no seating at an island, there is no extra requirement for the seated person, so the distance required between the edge of the island and the nearest obstruction may be reduced slightly to about 36 inches. However, between an island and other working cabinets, or between an island and appliances, there should always be 45 to 48 inches of clear space for island use and ease of circulation.

Peninsulas

These three-sided islands with their fourth side attached to other cabinets or a kitchen wall are space hogs just like islands, especially when they have seating. The same rules of spacing mentioned for islands and tables apply to peninsulas.

Since they usually run at right angles to the two main walls of your kitchen (across the short direction), leaving enough room at the end of the peninsula for one or two people to easily pass by is critical. Keep in mind you will walk past the end with food and drinks in your hand all the time. Do not squeeze that opening, you need a minimum of 36 inches clear (preferably 45 to 48 inches like with tables and islands).

You can have seating on the non-kitchen side of your peninsula. You could also sit at the narrow end just leave enough clearance from the back of those stools or chairs when you designate the circulation space for the peninsula.

Pantry Closets

Pantries require a lot of space to store your dry goods and small appliances.

Traditionally we stored kitchen goods in pantry closets of differing sizes. But closets are hard to outfit with logical storage systems that maximize storage capacity. They typically waste a lot of floorspace too.

In larger, luxury kitchens, large walk-in pantries are still very common if they can be placed adjacent to the kitchen.

But in more modest-sized kitchens, pantry cabinets are a far more useful and productive storage method. They are super-efficient at storing all-sized goods on roll-out trays below eye level, and on a couple shelves above eye level. They come in many widths, and you can use more than one. They waste nothing on floorspace and require the same 24 inches of front clearance that any other kitchen cabinet needs.

They are not inexpensive (three to five times the cost of a single base cabinet), but they are very space efficient and a better deal than a space-wasting closet type pantry.

Pantry cabinets typically come with four lower roll-out trays, but you can order additional roll-outs and customize your storage based on the heights needed on every shelf.

Because these cabinets are bulky and large, they are often combined with refrigerators and wall ovens in a storage/appliance wall so all your dry/cold/frozen goods are stored in one convenient location against a solid wall, freeing up the rest of the kitchen to be more open and airy.

Refrigerators and Freezers

These are typically recessed between cabinets or possibly built into a wall, so there's only one side of them we need to concern ourselves with—the front. This is obviously the case, since their doors and drawers pull out into what is typically circulation space.

To properly space cabinets, tables, or islands away from the front of your refrigerator/freezer (whether combined in one appliance, or as two appliances) you need to leave the same 45 to 48 inches as with tables and islands so that the open doors or drawers of the fridge do not stop passing traffic.

Additionally, the 45 or 48 inches are measured from the front of the refrigerator, not the cabinets next to it. This is because most traditional refrigerators stick out 7 to 9 inches beyond the face of the cabinets beside them.

This becomes even more important if you have a single hinged refrigerator door, and not french or side-by-side doors, since it projects about 35 inches out from the refrigerator, totally blocking the circulation path. In this case, the space to the next obstruction would be increased to 54 inches or more to allow someone to pass with the single refrigerator door open.

The final placement issue with regard to refrigerators and freezers (as well as wall oven and pantry cabinets) is that they should typically go together on a solid wall of the kitchen, and not along the rear sink wall that has a window and or door in it. If placed in that location, their bulk will block sight lines and light on both sides and provide a blockage point at the entry to the working portion of the kitchen. So always try to locate them on an interior, solid wall.

Commercial Ranges & Cooktops

These items are all sized larger than traditional ranges and often have more burners, larger ovens, and matching extra-large vent hoods.

It's easy to imagine more than one cook at the range, so be sure to leave enough space for the cook to stand at the range and still have someone pass easily behind them with their hands full. This means a minimum obstruction free distance of 48 inches between the face of the range or cooktop and any cabinets, island, or table.

You will routinely be carrying hot, heavy loads to and from the range, oven, and cooktop, so be sure that action is not hindered by squeezing the amount of space in front of the appliance too small for someone to pass when the oven is open.

Walkways and Circulation

While circulation space is not a physical thing in your kitchen, it is critical none the less. Floorspace in any kitchen that is not filled with cabinets, storage, windows, appliances, and eating functions is used for moving about.

Think of the space designated for circulation as hallways. True, there are no walls, but the cabinets, islands, appliances, and tables act like walls. And you need to leave plenty of room for folks to pass one another with groceries or hot food. This is in addition to the space needed to use your Space Hogs and cabinets!

The reason I have used 48 inches between obstructions is that the typical human male is about 22 inches from side to side. Give him an inch on either side, so he's not rubbing against something, and you're at 24 inches. Double that so two people can pass each other with an armload of groceries or hot food, and you have my magic 48-inch dimension.

Pro Tip:

Most remodelers and bad designers will try to space your tables, islands and peninsulas closer together than I have suggested. They will tell you that you will get "more kitchen" if you drop to 39-inch spacing between obstacles. Don't do it. Forget it.

You can't place kitchen obstacles closer than 45 inches and still have a fully-functional kitchen. If you try to squeeze it, you'll regret it for years. There's no point investing $40,000 or more in a new kitchen and ending up with regrets.

If you want a kitchen that works, stick with the 45 to 48 inches as the minimum spacing between all obstacles and you'll adore your new kitchen.

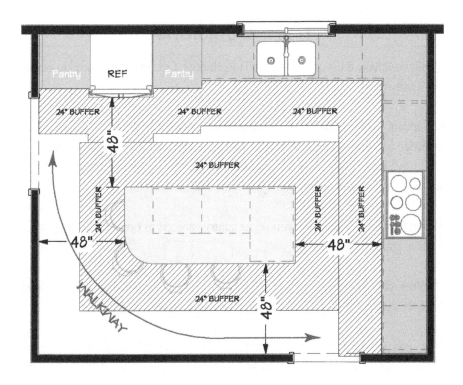

Remember, people love to encroach and hang out while you're making a meal or a dessert. Leaving a few more inches as I suggest means you can still move around freely without their presence blocking your way.

These extra few inches I call for make the difference between a custom solution that is a delight to use and an okay kitchen. You deserve the custom solution. So hold the line on kitchen obstacle spacing and you'll fall in love with your new kitchen again each time you use it.

Refer back to the spacing illustration displayed in the "Tables with Chairs and Eating Islands" section for a clearer understanding of the reasons for these spacing dimensions.

If you follow the spacing guidelines in this chapter when you make your Space Hog decisions, you'll enjoy the benefits for twenty years to come!

Hard Decisions

It's time to make a list of your Space Hog choices. Get rid of all Space Hogs you don't truly need.

Redundant seating is the most common abuse of space in kitchens, and deciding to forego a table and chairs or island seating is a difficult decision. But when you do it now, before you meet the first designer or remodeler, it costs you nothing and saves you lots of stress, money, and time down the road.

The same thing is true when you select pantry cabinets as opposed to a step-in or walk-in pantry.

Or when you choose a conventional range over a cooktop and wall ovens. You not only save a lot of space, but several thousand dollars.

Now you get to decide which things will be in your kitchen. It's not your responsibility to arrange them or design a solution–the pros will do that. It's your job to let them know which parts and pieces they will be working with.

It's so much easier to wrestle with this for a little while now than to get stressed and frustrated when you have an architect or designer pushing you for answers.

Update Your Table Once Again

Now that we have covered the biggest space hogs, you are able to make informed decisions about which style of cooking, storage types, and eating locations for your new kitchen. so, as before, add this new information to the Kitchen Selection Table in your Project Packet so it all gets to your designers and remodelers.

Chapter 33

Final Thoughts

You now have at your disposal all the tools needed to successfully plan and coordinate your professional kitchen renovation.

You can properly perform the following nine tasks:
- Prepare a complete Project Packet.
- Choose the right design professional if you need one.
- Identify the right type of remodeler to interview.
- Thoroughly interview your selected remodelers.
- Review their remodeling designs and proposals carefully.
- Select the best remodeler for your needs.
- Negotiate your best possible final price.
- Review your remodeling contract.
- Sign up and begin your new kitchen remodeling project!

Eliminate Costly Mistakes

There are many mistakes folks make when they remodel. But three of them tend to derail projects and cost thousands of extra dollars to overcome. Avoiding these mistakes is not difficult; you just need to understand what they are and follow the process laid out in the book.

1. Never start the remodeling process without being fully prepared.
2. Don't choose the wrong remodeler (specialization or type).
3. Don't select your remodeler based on lowest price.

Put on the right remodeling mindset at the start and keep it on. Be the Boss throughout the process, and remain in control of your project.

Perform your role well by hiring an excellent employee to work for you. Then step back and let them do what you hired them to do: design and construct an awesome new kitchen project that adds value to your home and brings you improved function, beauty, and delight every day for years to come.

Remodel With Confidence!

———

"We all deserve a home we love and are proud to show off."

Jim Molinelli

THE REMODELING PROFESSOR

If you liked

Remodel Your Kitchen!

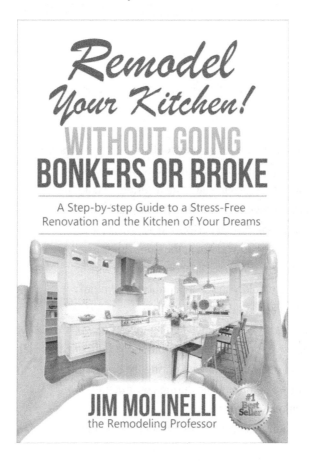

Please leave a brief **review** on

It's very helpful for the next homeowner!

Appendix 1

Remodeler Interview Questions

Here are some recommended questions to ask when you interview traditional remodelers.

- Please provide proof of insurance [liability + workers' comp]
- Please provide 3 references with similar size jobs.
- Please arrange a jobsite visit with a current client
- What is your total revenue in a typical year? [1]
- How many jobs do you perform in a typical year? [1]
- How many jobs do you run at the same time?
- Do you use employees or subcontracted crews?
- Which subs would you use in a project like mine?
- What hours & days do you work?
- How long is it from contract signing to start of work?
- Have you ever been to court or arbitration? [Circumstances?]
- Who will I communicate with during the design phase?
- How will we communicate during construction?
- Do you allow Change Orders?
- Are there administrative charges for change orders?

[1] These two questions help determine average project size.

Download your copy at:
www.RemodelingProfessor.com/RYK20

Appendix 2

Remodeler Scorecard

Use this Remodeler Scorecard when you are
evaluating and ranking your remodelers.
Grab a copy today!

REMODELER SCORECARD								
Remodeler Name	Qualifications	Professionalism	Design	Proposal	Preference	Price	References	TOTAL SCORE
A								
B								
C								
D								
E								

© 2020 Jim Molinelli LLC

Download your copy at:
www.RemodelingProfessor.com/RYK20

Appendix 3

Project Start-Up Workbook

This free download will help as you begin your Project Packet

It is literally a sample Project Packet with notes, instructions, and worksheets for each section.

Download your free copy at:
www.RemodelingProfessor.com/RYK20

Ask Me Anything!

Sometimes…
you still have questions or concerns,
even after reading a book like this.

Now you can…

Ask the

Remodeling Professor!

Jim offers **1-on-1 video coaching calls** and
gives **clear answers and action steps**
for your specific situation!

---

*Jim is an impartial remodeling expert,
a life-long industry insider, and
his only interest is your success!*

SCHEDULE YOUR CALL NOW:

www.RemodelingProfessor.com/call

About the Author

Jim Molinelli is the Remodeling Professor. He has earned three architecture degrees and holds a Maryland architectural license. He also taught on the architecture faculty at Texas A&M University.

Jim then spent the next 24 years in the design-build remodeling field helping Maryland families improve their homes and improve their lives. His unique designs have garnered more than fifty remodeling awards. He also received the Maryland Governor's Citation for Meritorious Service twice: in 2006 and 2016.

In 2002, he created and started teaching 'Prepare to Remodel' classes for homeowners through the local college. Those led to his first bestseller *Remodel! Without Going Bonkers or Broke* and his innovative video remodeling courses for homeowners. He also offers 1-on-1 video remodeling coaching.

He and his family live in the suburban Washington, DC area. He enjoys travel and golf and is an avid baseball fan.

Jim also does occasional live workshops, classes, home shows, and speaking engagements. You can contact Jim through his website:

Made in the USA
Middletown, DE
12 May 2024

54242166R00139